Belgium

Belgium

BY MICHAEL BURGAN

Enchantment of the World
Second Series

Children's Press®

A Division of Grolier Publishing

NEW YORK   LONDON   HONG KONG   SYDNEY
DANBURY, CONNECTICUT

Frontispiece: Children dressed for Mardi Gras in Binche

Consultant: Linda Cathryn Everstz, Ph.D., University of California, Berkeley

Please note: All statistics are as up-to-date as possible at the time of publication.

Visit Children's Press on the Internet: http://publishing.grolier.com

Book Production by Herman Adler Design Group

Library of Congress Cataloging-in-Publication Data

Burgan, Michael
    Belgium / by Michael Burgan.
      p. cm. — (Enchantment of the world. Second series)
    Summary: Describes the geography, plants and animals, history,
economy, language, religions, culture, sports and arts, and people
of Belgium.
    ISBN 0-516-21006-8
    1. Belgium—Juvenile literature. [1. Belgium.] I. Title.
II. Series.
DH418.B87 2000
949.3—dc21   99-21338
                                                        CIP
                                                         AC

GROLIER
PUBLISHING

Acknowledgments

The author would like to thank Liliane Opsomer of the Belgian Tourist Office; Tim and Nathalie Boullion; Martine Wauters and Daniel Brandt of Brussels; and Halley Gatenby at Children's Press.

Cover photo:
Bruges

Contents

Ghent

Fishing on horseback

One Nation, Two Cultures

A canal in the city of Tournai

A TRAVELER BOARDS THE TRAIN IN BRUGES, BELGIUM. She leaves behind the city's picturesque buildings and canals, heading for the nearby city of Tournai. Not sure if she's on the right train, she turns to another passenger. He assures her the train is going to Doornik.

Doornik? The woman is confused. She asked about Tournai. Where is Doornik? The man apologizes with a smile. Doornik is Tournai, to a person like himself, who speaks Flemish. To an American, or to a French-speaking Belgian, the city is called Tournai. Across Belgium, the cities and towns often have two names: one in French, the other in Flemish. Both languages are spoken in this tiny country. (A third language, German, is also used in a small corner of Belgium close to Germany.)

Belgium is almost like two countries in one. In the north is the region of Flanders, home of the Belgian people called Flemings. Their language, Flemish, is a form of Dutch. The two languages look almost the same when written, but some words are pronounced differently. And even within Flanders, there are local dialects of Flemish. The Flemings call their

Opposite: **A canal in Bruges**

A bilingual road sign in Brussels

country "Belgie." In the south is Wallonia, where most people speak French and are called Walloons. To them, Belgium is "La Belgique."

In the heart of Flanders is Belgium's capital, Brussels. Flemings call it Brussel, while French-speakers say Bruxelles. Despite its location in Flanders, the city has a large French-speaking population—about 80 percent. The city is officially bilingual, so street names and signs are posted in both languages.

Regional and National Identity

People who are born in one region of Belgium might live or work in the other. Many Belgians, however, continue to identify with the culture and language of their home region. Sometimes their loyalty is even stronger for their hometown than for the region. Language and cultural differences play a large part in Belgium's politics. In the past, Flemish- and French-speakers even fought in the streets over the right to use their own language.

Today, the two sides live peacefully together, in Brussels and throughout Belgium. But some tensions remain. Some Belgians—as well as some foreigners—sometimes question if a distinct country called Belgium really exists. Maybe it is just two separate regions with distinct languages that happen to share similar histories and the same king.

Other Belgians, however, do see a distinct national identity, separate from their regional roots. Belgians in both Flanders and Wallonia take pride in their country's great artistic history.

BELGIUM

- ● Provincial capitals
- ● Cities of over 100,000 people
- ○ Smaller cities and towns
- ⊱──── Canals

0 ────── 40 miles

0 ────── 60 kilometers

North
Sea

N E T H E R L A N D S

N
W ✦ *E*
S

G E R M A N Y

Antwerp

○ Deurne

ANTWERP

Bruges

EAST FLANDERS

Heusden

○ Mechelen

Hasselt

FLANDERS ● Ghent

Ath ○

○ Aalst

Albert
Canal

WEST FLANDERS

Anderlecht

Brussels

○ Louvain

Tongeren

LIMBURG

○ Ypres

Halle ○

BRABANT

Liège

Charleroi Canal

Tournai

HAINAUT

Liberchies

Namur

Meuse

WALLONIA

Ourthe

LIÈGE

○ Durbuy

● Mons

Binche ○

Charleroi

NAMUR

Maas

Maas

St. Hubert ○

Bastogne

LUXEMBOURG

Semois

LUXEMBOURG

Arlon ●

FRANCE

BELGIUM

Teens meeting in the streets of Bruges

They share a love of fine foods and Belgium's national beverage, beer. Belgians of every background cherish their family and friendships. Flemings and Walloons alike share the benefits of Belgium's modern economy while appreciating customs that are centuries old.

Shaped by History

Belgium's unique history led to the development of its two cultures. Located in the center of western Europe, Belgium was often controlled and influenced by its larger neighbors. These foreign rulers have included ancient Romans, the French, Spaniards, Austrians, and the Dutch. Some people say that the centuries of foreign control have shaped the personality of the Belgian people.

A busy pedestrian shopping street in Brussels

Until the nineteenth century, foreigners ruled the Belgians. Under these foreign rulers, many Belgians questioned authority and tried to find ways to bend rules. Some Belgians today joke that trying to avoid paying taxes is a national sport. Foreign rule also taught Belgians how to make compromises rather than fight. They still respect the need to find peaceful solutions to personal and political arguments. That's why the Flemings and the Walloons have been able to live together.

No matter who ruled them, Belgians have always been hard workers. They first made their country a center for commerce hundreds of years ago. Belgium still plays that role today. And because of the many centuries of control by outsiders, Belgians appreciate independence and democracy. Today Belgians work hard to keep their democratic system fair for all.

The World Comes to Belgium

Belgium's position at the "crossroads of Europe" gives the country an international flavor. This is especially true in Brussels. The city has offices for many foreign companies. It is also the home of the North Atlantic Treaty Organization (NATO). This organization was created primarily by the United States after World War II. NATO is a military alliance with members from nineteen European and North American nations. Belgium is also the major gathering spot of the European Union (EU). The EU represents fifteen countries that have joined together to promote their economic strength. EU representatives meet in Brussels, adding to its worldly air.

Leaders from many countries gather at a NATO meeting.

Belgians are comfortable with the foreigners who visit and work in their country. They have also come to accept the linguistic and cultural differences between their own ethnic groups. They have blended their old traditions with the conveniences of modern life. Belgium is small, but its people have offered the world many things. The country delights all those who take the time to explore it.

Flatlands and Forests

O<small>N</small> B<small>ELGIUM'S</small> <small>COAST</small> <small>ALONG</small> <small>THE</small> N<small>ORTH</small> S<small>EA,</small> <small>VACA-</small>
tioners come to swim on sandy beaches. At the other end of
Belgium, the Ardennes features rugged, tree-covered peaks. In
between, Belgium is a nation of flatlands and marshy forests.

Children play with starfish near the sea at Ostend.

The Heart of Western Europe

The distance between the North Sea and the farthest edge
of the Belgian Ardennes marks the longest distance in this tiny
country—about 174 miles (280 km). The land between these
two extremes is dotted with farms, bustling modern cities, and
rivers that help link Belgium to the rest of Europe. The country's
position in the middle of western Europe has made it a center for
trade and commerce. Human efforts, such as the building of
canals and dikes, have also shaped Belgium's landscape.

Opposite: **A farmhouse in the Ardennes**

Belgium's Geographical Features

Area: 11,781 square miles (30,510 sq km)

Population Density: 871 persons per square mile (336 per sq km)

Largest City: Brussels metro region, population 950,597 (1997)

Highest Elevation: Signal de Botrange, in the Ardennes, 2,277 feet (694 m)

Lowest Point: The North Sea, sea level

Geographical Center: Oignies-en-Thierache, Namur province

Average Daily Temperatures (Brussels):
 37°F (3°C) in January
 64°F (18°C) in July

Average Annual Precipitation: 28 inches (71 cm) near the sea; more than 40 inches (102 cm) in the Ardennes

Oldest Town: Tongeren (founded in first century A.D.)

Longest River: Meuse, 560 miles (901 km)

Belgium covers 11,781 square miles (30,510 sq km), making it slightly larger than the state of Maryland. It borders France to the south and west, the Netherlands to the north, and Germany to the east. The tiny country of Luxembourg is on Belgium's southeastern border. Belgium's only natural borders are a 42-mile (68-km) stretch of coast along the North Sea in the northwest, and a tiny section of the Meuse River that separates Belgium and the Netherlands. The rest of

Belgium's borders are jagged lines and sweeping curves through the land. Centuries of wars and shifting control by foreign powers helped create these borders. Within Belgium, the country has three major geographic regions: the lowlands, the central plateau, and the Ardennes.

The Lowlands

Belgium, the Netherlands, and Luxembourg are sometimes called the Low Countries. This nickname comes from the region's mostly flat terrain. Starting at the North Sea, Belgium's lowlands continue inland to the Schelde River. The land never reaches an elevation greater than 300 feet (91 m) above sea level. The area closest to the sea is the flattest and is known

Colorful shops line the streets at *Vrijdagmarkt*, or Friday market, in Ghent.

Land from the Sea

In the eighth century, Belgians began to build canals near the North Sea. These canals drained off seawater, providing new land for the people to farm. In some cases, windmills helped pump the water into the canals. These strips of land reclaimed from the sea are called *polders*. Polders make up about 10 percent of Belgium's land area.

Sand dunes up to 65 feet (20 m) high help keep the coastal waters from flooding the polders. The dunes are often hidden from view, with buildings and roads built on top of them. In some places, Belgians have built concrete dikes to prevent floods from the sea. The Belgian coast features resorts and beaches. Ostend, the largest resort town on the North Sea, was once called "Queen of the Belgian Coast."

Despite human and natural barriers between the water and the low-lying land, flooding is still a threat along the coast.

for its polders, strips of land reclaimed from the sea. The largest cities in this region are Ghent and Bruges. Both feature canals and well-preserved medieval buildings.

The lowlands of Belgium's northwest also extend to the east, in a region called Kempenland. Bordering the Netherlands, this area features woods, ponds, and marshes. In general, the sandy soil in Kempenland is not good for farming. The region relies on mining and industry for its economy. Antwerp, Belgium's second-largest city, is on the southern edge of Kempenland.

The town of Dinant on the Meuse River

The Central Plateau

Farther inland, the terrain slowly begins to rise. Rich soil in this central region makes it Belgium's most productive farmland. Brussels, the capital, is centrally located in this region. The central plateau is bordered by the Sambre-Meuse river valley. This 100-mile- (161-km-) long valley was once the site of heavy coal mining and other industries. Many of Wallonia's most important cities developed along the Meuse, including Liège, Charleroi, and Namur.

Looking at Belgium's Cities

Antwerp, located on the Schelde River, is the second-busiest port in Europe. It is the capital of the province of the same name. With about 453,000 people, Antwerp is Belgium's second-largest city. It is famous as one of the world's great diamond trading and cutting centers. Charlemagne, a great French ruler of the eighth century, built the first fort in Antwerp. A fortress dating to the tenth century, the Steen, still stands in the city's harbor. Another famous landmark is the Onze Lieve Vrouwekathedraal (Cathedral of Our Lady). It is the largest church in Belgium built in the Gothic style. Gothic churches feature huge towers, called spires, and massive windows. Inside, the Onze Lieve Vrouwekathedraal houses great works of art by a master Flemish painter, Peter Paul Rubens (1577–1640).

Ghent, located northwest of Brussels on a group of islands, is the capital of the province of East Flanders. It was once one of the most important commercial centers in Europe. Ghent's wealth came from the textile, or cloth, trade. Today, this city of about 225,000 people is a major port with steel and chemical factories as well as textile mills. Ghent is filled with stunning old buildings. Its history goes back to around the seventh century, when monks built two abbeys near the present site of the city. Like Antwerp, Ghent's churches contain masterpieces of Flemish art. The castle of the counts of Flanders (below, left) was built in the twelfth century.

Charleroi (population 204,899) and Liège (pop. 189,510) are the largest cities in Wallonia. Liège is also the capital of the province of Liège. These cities were once the heart of Belgium's coal and steel industries, but recently they have lost jobs to industries in Flanders. Of the two cities, Liège is the more popular tourist destination, because of its palace and its famous churches dating to the eleventh century.

Bruges is the smallest of Belgium's best-known cities, with a population of about 115,000. It serves as the capital of the province of West Flanders. The old center section of the city has well-preserved medieval buildings and canals that draw many tourists. Bruges was founded by one of the great early rulers of Flanders, Baldwin Iron-Arm. He resisted the power of the French and made himself the Count of Flanders. Baldwin kidnapped the French king's daughter and made her his wife. He fortified the area near Bruges in the ninth century. Centuries later, thanks to the cloth trade, Bruges became one of northern Europe's wealthiest cities. Today, the city's center features the old Markt, or marketplace, and the oldest town hall in Belgium.

Hands Down

A statue in the center of Antwerp pays tribute to a Roman soldier named Silvius Brabo. According to a local legend, Brabo's heroics led to the city's name.

The legend says that a giant named Druon Antigon once guarded the Schelde River. Antigon demanded a toll from ships as they passed his castle. If a captain refused, the giant cut off the captain's hand and threw it into the river. Brabo fought and killed the giant, and then cut off Antigon's hand and threw it into the river. *Hand-werpen* is Flemish for "hand-throwing," and so the city was named for this famous incident.

Although this story is still talked about, most people realize it's not true. Antwerp's name actually comes from the Flemish word *aanwerpen*, meaning "raised ground." The city was founded on a strip of land that rose out of the river.

The Ardennes

Moving eastward from the Sambre-Meuse Valley, the Belgian countryside becomes hilly. This region is the Ardennes, Belgium's least-populated area. The hills of the Ardennes gradually become small mountains. The tallest peaks are found near the German border. Belgium's highest elevation, the Signal de Botrange, is located here. This area is also home to most of Belgium's German-speaking population. The region was part of Germany until 1919.

The Ardennes features thick forests and rocky cliffs. The beautiful scenery and opportunities for outdoor sports make it

a popular recreation area. The land, however, is not very good for farming, except for one small area. This region, called Belgian Lorraine, borders a part of France also called Lorraine. Forestry is an important industry in the region, as is tourism.

Countryside in the Ardennes

Medicinal Mud

In the Ardennes is the resort town of Spa, famous for its water and mud. The Romans first noted that the waters around Spa seemed to have healing powers. In the sixteenth century, Europe's richest citizens started coming to Spa to rest and socialize with each other. Spa became so popular its name was used to describe any health resort with mineral waters.

Today, visitors still come for the baths. The mud baths are heated to about 100°F (38°C). The mud, which looks like melted chocolate, is smooth and creamy. After taking a mud bath, guests shower and then go for a refreshing dip in the mineral water. Minerals in the water and mud are said to have medicinal powers. Spa's baths are supposed to help relieve sore joints and muscles and heal other ailments.

Durbuy was once considered the smallest city in the world.

The towns in the Ardennes tend to be far apart and rather small. One of the better-known towns is Durbuy, which features a castle built in the eleventh century. Arlon, with a population of about 23,000, is one of the largest towns in the heart of the Ardennes. The town was built on an old Roman settlement, and a stone tower from Roman times still stands.

Belgium's Rivers

For centuries, Belgium's rivers have moved goods and people throughout the country and into neighboring nations. The most important waterway is the Meuse River. It starts in eastern France and enters Belgium in the Ardennes. At the city of Namur, the Sambre joins the Meuse. It then continues across Belgium and into the

Keeping the Names Straight

Here are the French and Flemish names for some of Belgium's major cities.

English	Flemish	French
Antwerp	Antwerpen	Anvers
Bruges	Brugge	Bruges
Brussels	Brussel	Bruxelles
Ghent	Gent	Gand
Liège	Luik	Liège

Netherlands. At some points, the Meuse is too shallow for ships, so canals have been cut through the land. In all of Europe, the only river more important for transportation than the Meuse is the Rhine in Germany.

Belgium's second great river is the Schelde. This 270-mile- (435-km-) long river begins in northern France and then cuts through Flanders on its way to the Netherlands and the North Sea. Antwerp was built along the banks of the Schelde, and Ghent lies near small branches of this river and the smaller Leie. Other small rivers in Belgium include the Semois and the Ourthe, both of which flow through the Ardennes.

A boat unloads passengers from a trip on the Schelde in Antwerp.

People use bridges to cross Belgium's canals.

Canals are also important waterways in Belgium. Canals link Bruges and Ghent to the North Sea. Another one connects Brussels to the Sambre River. Belgium's longest canal, the Albert, cuts through Kempenland, linking Liège and smaller cites to Antwerp.

A Moderate Climate

Belgium has what meteorologists call a temperate, or moderate, climate. The weather is rarely extremely hot or extremely cold. Within the country, however, there are regional differences. Along the coast, summer temperatures tend to be cooler than they are farther inland. During the winter, the two regions have similar temperatures. Both the lowlands and the central region are often covered with fog, and rain is common in the spring and fall. The coastal regions average about 28 inches (71 cm) of rain per year, with about 210 days having some rain. In the United States, the Pacific Coast, from northern California to Washington, has a similar climate.

Belgium's greatest weather extremes occur in the Ardennes. There, the summers are a little cooler than in the central region. In the winter, the mountainous region is especially cold. The average January temperature is 24.4°F (-4.2°C), a few degrees colder than in the rest of the country. The Ardennes receives the majority of Belgium's snow. Snow falls on an average of 50 days each winter.

Pollution Problems

Pollution of all kinds is a problem in Belgium, as it is in many European nations. Belgium's chemical plants and other factories create high levels of air pollution. Rivers and the North Sea are polluted by industrial waste and by fertilizer used on crops. To fight the problem, Belgium passed tougher antipollution laws. One of these restricted the dumping of toxic wastes. Belgium also signed a number of international treaties designed to help the environment. These include agreements to reduce chemicals that harm the ozone and to protect endangered animals.

Despite these efforts to clean up the environment, pollution is still a problem in the Meuse River. In the past, waste from steel production was dumped in the river. In 1996, an environmental group, the World Wide Fund for Nature, launched a plan to buy remaining natural land along the river. By buying the land, the group hoped to prevent new industrial development along the river. This would help reduce future pollution and preserve the plants and animals that live near the Meuse.

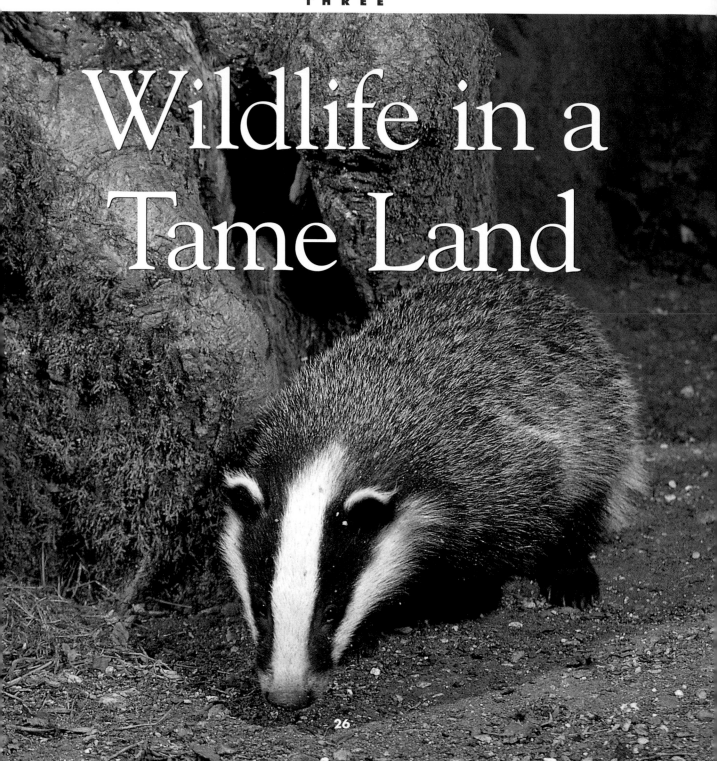

Wildlife in a Tame Land

C ITY LIFE DEVELOPED EARLY WITHIN BELGIUM'S BORders, as people built homes and industries. Today, the country's growth has spread from the cities to nearby suburbs. After centuries of development, Belgians have cut down many of the forests that were once home to birds and animals. And fields where wildflowers once bloomed have been cleared. But Belgium still has areas of natural beauty where wild animals and plants thrive.

Opposite: **A badger searching for food**

Lily of the valley

Life in the Forest and Field

Kempenland, in Belgium's northeast corner, is covered with marshy land. Though crops don't grow well there, the region is heavily forested with coniferous trees. These are trees with cones, such as pine. Within these forests are many animals that are also common in North America, such as squirrels, rabbits, and deer.

Most other forests in Belgium feature deciduous trees—trees that shed their leaves in the fall—such as elm, birch, and beech. Belgium's most common deciduous tree is the oak. Flowers found across Belgium include hyacinth, goldenrod, lily of the valley, and digitalis. Leaves from the digitalis are dried and used as a medicine to treat heart ailments.

A marten leaps from a tree.

The country's largest forest region is the Ardennes. This forest has a mixture of deciduous and coniferous trees. In the Ardennes mountains wild boars roam. The boars are a favorite target for hunters, and boar meat often turns up on dinner tables. Other animals of the Ardennes include foxes, wildcats, and tree martens, relatives of the weasel. North of the Ardennes, the wildlife includes muskrats and hamsters.

In the eastern edge of the Ardennes, and extending into Germany, are swamps known as fens—*fagnes* in French. The Haute Fagnes Nature Park is located there, and it is a popular spot for hikers and other nature lovers. The area has a variety of trees, wild grasses, and heather. Animals in the region include hinds—a type of deer—otters, badgers, and ermines. Another relative of the weasel, ermines are prized for their fur, which turns pure white in winter.

A brown bear

Some animals that used to roam freely in the Ardennes are now rare. Many of these animals now live within the wildlife reserve in Han-sur-Lesse. Visitors there see bison, brown bears, and wild horses in their natural surroundings.

The Coast

Belgium's North Sea coast is home to a variety of waterbirds. Many of them live at the Het Zwin Nature Reserve. The reserve is located at the mouth of a river that once led to Bruges. Over time, the port filled with silt, cutting Bruges off from the sea. Now the site has Belgium's largest salt marsh and a bird sanctuary. Birds that live along the coast include geese, storks, lapwings, white plovers, gulls, and ducks. Many birds also stop along the beaches to rest as they fly south for the winter.

Nearby is Westhoek Nature Reserve. This park preserves about 840 acres (340 ha) of sand dunes. This stretch of dunes has been called Belgium's Sahara. Human activity, combined with wind and water, threatens the existence of dunes like these all over the world. The dunes along the Belgian coast also feature wildflowers. In summer, stretches of sea lavender cover the seaside in purple.

Going Batty

As in other countries, some wild animals in Belgium face extinction. Several species of bats are endangered. In 1994, the Belgian branch of the World Wide Fund for Nature conducted studies of bats to learn where they roosted, so that these sites could be preserved. The group also tried to educate Belgians about bats. Many people think bats are harmful to humans, but actually they're helpful. One bat can eat thousands of insects in a single night, including such harmful bugs as mosquitoes.

For the Birds

Belgians must love their birds. In addition to the Het Zwin bird sanctuary, Belgium is also home to the largest aviary (bird zoo) in Europe. The Parc Paradisio, in Cambron-Casteau, covers 32,293 square feet (3,000 sq m) and features more than 2,500 birds. The park is located on the grounds of a former abbey erected in the thirteenth century and includes three lakes and a small river.

Paradisio has native birds of Belgium as well as more exotic species from around the world. These foreign guests include ostriches, penguins, and parrots. The park has an enclosed building that is 300 feet

(91 m) long where some of the larger birds can fly at their leisure. Others live along the lakes and in the trees. These trees include Oriental plantains that are more than 300 years old.

Fishers in Oostduinkerke still ride into the water on horses to catch shrimp and fish.

Creatures of the River and the Sea

In the waters of the North Sea live more than forty types of fish, including shellfish. Many of these fish end up in some of Belgium's famous national dishes. Shrimp, mussels, eel, sole, and turbot are among the fish found in the North Sea. In Oostduinkerke, fishers still use the traditional method for catching shellfish: They ride into the water on horses and snare the fish in nets. Belgium's rivers also have a number of freshwater fish, such as pike and trout.

A Trip to the Zoo

Belgium's largest zoo is located in the heart of Antwerp. More than 150 years old, the Antwerp Zoo is one of the oldest zoos in Europe. Along with animals from around the world, the zoo has an aquarium, a reptile house, a park where deer roam, and a museum of natural history. The zoo's *nocturama* features nocturnal animals—creatures that sleep by day and hunt at night.

Some of the zoo's more popular residents are the dolphins, which perform for visitors, and polar bears. Many of the animals at the Antwerp Zoo live in open settings similar to their native habitats.

Keeping Brussels Green

The land around Brussels was once covered with fields, forests, and marshes. Over the centuries, humans cut down the trees for firewood and cleared the land for buildings. Since the 1980s, the government has tried to preserve what remains of this open space and the animals that live there.

Green spaces covered with grass and trees are not just pretty scenery. Forests like the Soignes help keep the air clean. Plants and trees consume carbon dioxide, the gas people emit when they exhale. Too much carbon dioxide in the air is not good for the planet. Preserving forests helps ensure Earth's health.

At the Soignes, local residents pitch in to keep the forest clean. Teams of volunteers remove litter and help clean the ponds.

Green City

Although Brussels is a major city, it still has pockets of wildlife in and around it. Across the Charleroi Canal, just west of the city, are a string of parklands and nature reserves. The fields and marshlands of Scheutbos lead to woods filled with birds and insects. The nearby marshes of Jette and Ganshoren are home to kingfishers and herons, wading birds famous for their fishing skills.

On the southeast side of Brussels is the Soignes Forest, the largest forest in the region. About 80 percent of the Soignes is covered with beech trees, and squirrels and foxes live among them. The forest has five natural reserves, which feature ponds and hiking trails. A special garden in the forest is used to grow plants that may have uses in medicine.

A foggy day in the Soignes Forest

The Path to Nationhood

T ENS OF THOUSANDS OF YEARS AGO, HUMANS FIRST SETTLED in the area that is now Belgium. Many centuries passed before a more modern society developed there. And only since the nineteenth century have the people of Belgium ruled themselves in an independent nation. Belgium's location at the crossroads of Europe made it an easy target for foreign rulers and their armies. The history of Belgium has been shaped by these many outside influences, and by the Belgians' struggle to win their independence.

Celts and Romans

About 4,000 years ago, groups of fierce warriors swept across western Europe. These people, called the Celts, settled across the continent and in the British Isles. Over time, they forged weapons out of iron. They also built boats and traded with people who lived along the Mediterranean Sea to the south. One of these Celtic peoples was the Belgae. The word *Belgium* comes from their name.

By the first century B.C., the Romans dominated Europe. They expanded their territory through conquest, moving into a Celtic region known as Gaul. In 57 B.C., the great Roman general Julius Caesar led his troops into the land of the Belgae. In a series of quick battles, the Romans defeated the Belgae. Caesar, however, praised his opponents. "Of all the people of Gaul," he wrote, "the Belgae are the bravest."

Julius Caesar by Peter Paul Rubens

For nearly 500 years, the Romans ruled the region, and their culture blended with Celtic traditions. The Romans built roads that linked the Belgae with other parts of the Roman Empire. They also established Tongeren, the first Belgian town.

The Coming of the Franks

Around the third century A.D., another people arrived in the land of the Belgae. These were the Franks, a tribe from Germany, who settled in what is now Flanders. They spoke a Germanic language, which is the root of modern Dutch and Flemish. Meanwhile, in the Celtic areas, the Belgae were developing a new language that mixed their own tongue with the Latin spoken by the Romans. This language was later called French. The two distinct languages of Belgium were already taking shape.

Invasion of the Franks into Gaul

Early in the fifth century, the Roman Empire began to crumble. As Rome pulled its troops out of Belgium, more Franks poured in. Around 430, a Frankish leader named Claudine seized the city of Tournai. His great-grandson, Clovis, was born in that Belgian city.

Clovis expanded his family's holdings. In 481, he led an army of 6,000 troops into Gaul. Clovis's empire eventually stretched into part of Germany. During his rule, Clovis became the first Germanic king to convert to Christianity. Celtic monks from Ireland and Scotland brought the Christian religion to Belgium. In the seventh century, Belgians converted in great numbers and began to build monasteries across the land.

Clovis punishing an offender

Charlemagne and His Empire

The descendants of Clovis eventually lost control of their lands, and another Frankish dynasty emerged. A lord named Pepin the Short owned lands along the Meuse River, centered near Liège. His son, Charlemagne, became Europe's greatest leader during the early Middle Ages, a period that lasted roughly from the end of the fifth century to the tenth century. Described as tall, strong, and dignified, Charlemagne created an empire that included most of present-day France, Belgium, western Germany, the Netherlands, northern Italy, and Austria.

In 800, Charlemagne was crowned emperor by the pope, the leader of the Roman Catholic Church. The emperor's lands were described as a new Roman Empire. After Charlemagne's death, his empire was divided among his sons and grandsons. This empire never reached the importance of the Roman Empire.

Charlemagne

For the Belgians in the empire, life grew increasingly uncertain. Charlemagne's lands were split into three kingdoms. None of them was a strong military power. In the middle of the ninth century, invaders from Scandinavia began to attack Belgium and its neighbors. These fierce warriors were called Norsemen, or Vikings.

Sailing in small, fast, wooden ships, the Vikings struck hard at Belgium. They entered the Schelde, Meuse, and other rivers, and then destroyed churches, slaughtered citizens, and looted treasures. One Viking camp was at Louvain, just east of Brussels. Another was at Ghent. During these destructive attacks, Belgium did not have a strong ruler who could defend the people. Instead, the

Belgians had to ask local dukes and counts for protection. These wealthy landowners built castles and walls around towns. When the Norse invasions ended, around 900, these fortified towns and castles became the centers of Belgian life.

Good Fortunes Return

After the Norse invasions ended, the Belgians began to prosper. Along the North Sea, they built dikes to hold back the water and reclaim land for farming. Food production increased, thanks to new tools and better farming methods. More food led to a growth in population. Since fewer people were needed to farm the lands, more could become artisans and craftspeople.

Norsemen at Sea and Their Raven Pilot

Flanders had once had a simple industry based on making woolen cloth. The Norse invasions crushed that early trade, but it recovered in the tenth century. The Flemish cloth-makers eventually needed more raw wool than local farmers could produce, so they traded with England for wool. Skilled Flemish weavers wove cloth that was prized for its color and soft texture. Merchants sold the cloth across Europe and then used their profits to buy timber, furs, and grain.

Belgians on the Move

During the late Middle Ages, not all Belgians stayed home to help build a new economy. Many traveled to other parts of the world. Professional soldiers, called mercenaries, offered their services to foreign armies. Belgians fought for King William the Conqueror of Normandy when he invaded England in 1066. They also fought for the rulers of Byzantium, a Greek-speaking empire centered in what is now Istanbul, Turkey. Belgians were so respected for their fighting skills that at one time all European mercenaries were called *Brabancons*, referring to the Belgian region of Brabant.

Belgian priests and monks also traveled to help spread Christianity, reaching Poland and Russia. This tradition of missionary work continued into modern times.

Sometimes adventurous Belgians combined military service and religion. During the Crusades of the eleventh and twelfth centuries (right), many European nobles traveled to Jerusalem to battle the Muslims, who controlled that holy city. Ships bound for the Holy Land sailed from Ostend, on the North Sea. One of the great

Belgian crusaders was Godfrey of Bouillon, who became the first Christian ruler of Jerusalem.

Unlike the rest of Europe, the Flemish Belgians relied more on manufacturing and commerce than on farming to make their living. By the twelfth century, the cloth industry and the trades connected to it led to the growth of Ghent, Bruges, and Ypres. In the thirteenth century, Bruges was the commercial center of Europe. In the streets, a visitor might hear traders who spoke Spanish, English, French, Portuguese, or German. Bruges cloth was so cheap and well made, other countries could not compete with it.

A Battle for Flemish Pride

In the early thirteenth century, France won great influence in Flanders and wanted to make the region part of France. But the Flemings wanted no part of French rule. On May 18, 1302, the citizens of Bruges revolted against the French. The people ran through the city crying *"schild en vriendt,"* Flemish for "shield and friend." For someone who didn't speak Flemish, this slogan was difficult to say. Anyone in Bruges suspected of being French was slaughtered.

Two months later, the French struck back by sending a professional army to Flanders. The Flemings had only thirty knights leading a force of commoners, but they defeated the French near Courtrai. Legend has it that the Flemish collected 700 golden spurs from the fallen French knights, so the clash is known as the Battle of the Golden Spurs. Belgians in Flanders still celebrate this victory for Flemish independence.

The Rise of Burgundy

Although Belgium prospered in the fourteenth century, the region saw its share of troubles too. Armies from France often clashed with the Flemish. Workers sometimes fought each other for economic and political control. In 1347, a great plague, the Black Death, began sweeping across Europe. The plague would eventually kill up to one-third of the continent's adult population. Throughout this period, Belgium was still a collection of small states ruled by local nobles or powerful merchants. But in 1384, a royal family from Burgundy began to unite the Low Countries of Belgium and the Netherlands into one state.

In the fourteenth century, Burgundy was an independent nation in what is now eastern France. Philip the Bold, Duke of Burgundy, was married to the daughter of the Count of Flanders. Those family ties, however, did not stop Philip from leading his army against forces from Ghent. Philip eventually won control of almost all of Flanders and then inherited the

The Rebellious Merchant

In the fourteenth century, the Flemish weaving industry relied on English wool. In 1335, France and England went to war, with terrible results for the Flemish weavers. Flanders's rulers supported France, so England stopped shipping wool to the Flemish. As the Flemish weaving industry suffered, one man, Jacob van Artevelde, led a revolt against the pro-French rulers of Flanders.

Van Artevelde was a wealthy wool merchant from Ghent. He organized working people and other merchants to take power in that city. After England agreed to resume shipping wool, van Artevelde convinced the rest of Flanders to side with the English. Edward, the king of England, had a claim to be king of France. Thanks to van Artevelde's influence, Edward came to Ghent in 1340 and was proclaimed king of France.

But van Artevelde's influence did not last. Some people thought he had too close a relationship with Edward and wanted to turn Flanders over to England. In 1345, a crowd stormed van Artevelde's house and killed him. About forty years later, his son Philip led another popular uprising in Ghent, this time against the Count of Flanders.

title Count of Flanders from his father-in-law. Philip's rule marked the beginning of almost a century of great peace, prosperity, and artistic achievement in the Low Countries. These lands were sometimes called the Burgundian Netherlands.

Under the dukes of Burgundy, Belgium was part of one of the richest states in Europe. The most famous Burgundian duke was Philip III, known as Philip the Good, who ruled from 1419 to 1467. During his rule, the commercial heart of Europe switched from Bruges to Antwerp. Philip helped stir economic growth by promoting fairs in Antwerp, where merchants from all over Europe came to trade their goods. The Burgundian rulers also helped the city of Brussels grow by occasionally holding court there.

Philip III, Duke of Burgundy

Burgundian rule in Belgium ended in 1477. That year, Charles, the son of Philip the Good, died in battle. His daughter, Mary, then married Maximilian, a member of the powerful Hapsburg family from Austria. After Mary's death just a few years later, Maximilian tried to assert his control over the Low Countries. The Flemings in particular resisted Maximilian, but after a few years of fighting, the Belgians gave in to Hapsburg rule.

The Hapsburg empire reached its peak under Maximilian's grandson, Charles V. This future king of Spain was born in Ghent and grew up in the Belgian city of Mechelen. From his father's family, Charles inherited the Burgundian lands. From his mother, Charles took control of the vast Spanish lands, which included territory in Italy and colonies in the New World. By 1520, Charles ruled over more than 13 million Europeans.

Under Charles, the Low Countries were sometimes called the Spanish Lowlands, and they were at the center of European art and learning. But life was not always peaceful in Belgium. In 1540, the citizens of Ghent revolted to protest high taxes. Charles sent in troops to restore order. A new religious movement threatened the security of all of Europe's Catholic rulers, such as Charles. In 1517 named Martin Luther had cha'' pope and helped start Pr sometimes sent arm shiped in the fo son, Philip, Charles cretly wor- arfare came when his

Philip, once swore he would kill his own son become nt. In the Spanish to a variety of Protestan so held strong beliefs about indiv dom. Those beliefs posed another threat to a strong ruler lik Philip. Unlike his father, Philip had no ties to the Low Countries, and he did not hesitate to use force against the region's Protestants.

In the 1560s, some nobles urged Spain to tolerate the Protestants. Despite their efforts, Philip sent an army into Belgium in 1567. These troops arrested thousands of Protestants and executed many of them. Two of the condemned men, members of the Flemish nobility, were beheaded at the Brussels's marketplace. Many devout Protestants fled to Holland, where rebels fought for inde-

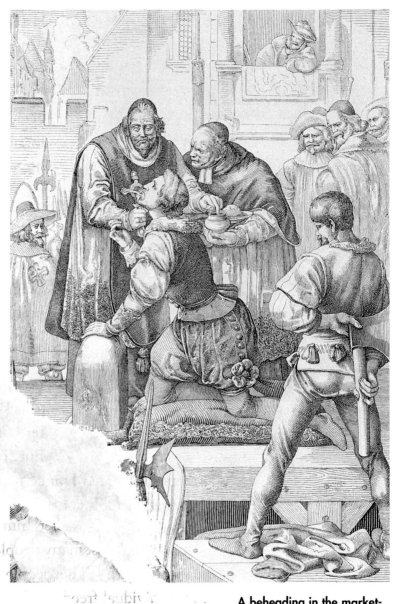

A beheading in the marketplace at Brussels in 1568

These

Provinc

in 1579.

The revolts in Belgium ended in 1585. Brussels became capital of a new region called the Spanish Netherlands—roughly the same territory as modern Belgium. Many Flemish Protestants fled Belgium to escape Spanish rule. The Netherlands remained a separate nation, though Spain did not recognize its independence until 1648. That was also the

Netherlands, 1609

United Netherlands
Spanish Netherlands

last year of the Thirty Years' War. Since 1618, political and religious conflict had spread throughout Europe. For the Low Countries, however, the bloody battles had gone on for almost eighty years. And the fighting was not over.

Europe's Battlefield

In the last half of the seventeenth century, France once again eyed Belgium, hoping to bring it under French rule. France fought the Netherlands, and later an alliance of European nations, in its effort to win Belgium. In 1695, French troops attacked Brussels, destroying the center of the city and some 4,000 homes. But by 1713, the other European powers had forced France to give up any claims to Belgium, and Austria took control of it. What had been the Spanish Netherlands was now the Austrian Netherlands.

In 1789, a revolution swept through France, ending the rule of kings. The Belgians were also touched by this spirit of independence and freedom. In 1790, the people proclaimed their independence from Austria and set up the United States of Belgium. The Austrian army, however, quickly ended this attempt at democratic rule. A few years later, Belgium was again influenced by events in France. In 1794, French forces defeated the Austrians near Charleroi. The next year, France took control of Belgium.

At first many Belgians welcomed the French. But over time the Belgians began to resent the French and their powerful leader, the great general Napoléon Bonaparte. Napoléon built a vast European empire, making him the enemy of England and Prussia. In 1815, forces from those two countries finally defeated Napoléon at the small Belgian town of Waterloo, just outside Brussels. The Belgians hoped they would finally win their independence. Instead, an alliance of

Napoléon and the Old Guard Before Waterloo **by Ernest Crofts**

European nations, influenced mainly by Great Britain, placed Belgium under Dutch control.

No one asked the Belgians about this arrangement. The Belgians expressed how they felt about their new rulers in songs and poems. "I am not a Dutchman," one song of the era went, "and I don't want to be." In 1830, the Belgians revolted against the Dutch. After the rebels defeated Dutch forces in Brussels, the Belgians declared their independence on October 4, 1830. The rest of Europe wanted to avoid another major war, so they officially recognized the new country in 1831.

Independent Belgium

In February 1831, the leaders of Belgium passed the country's first Constitution. The government they created had a parliament, elected by the wealthier citizens of the new nation. The government also had a king, but this king had to follow the wishes of Parliament. For their king, the Belgians chose Leopold I, a German prince and an uncle of England's Queen Victoria.

Under Leopold I, the Belgian economy grew. In 1835, Belgium opened the first public railway line in Europe. It also built modern factories to make steel and other goods. Belgium's growth continued under Leopold's son, Leopold II. When he took the throne in 1865, Leopold II said, "My ambition is to make Belgium greater, stronger, and more beautiful." For the most part, he succeeded.

Leopold II hired a great explorer named Henry Stanley to set up a Belgian colony in central Africa. This colony, called

The Kings of Belgium

Name	Length of Reign
Leopold I	1831–1865
Leopold II	1865–1909
Albert I	1909–1934
Leopold III	1934–1951
Baudouin I	1951–1993
Albert II	1993–

the Congo Free State (and later the Belgian Congo), sent valuable natural resources, such as diamonds, gold, and rubber, back to Belgium. Many people of the Congo Free State suffered under this rule. They were forced to endure long work hours, and some even died because of the severe treatment. Within Belgium, industry continued to grow, and Leopold ordered the building of great parks and public buildings.

The Two World Wars

Although small and relatively new, Belgium entered the twentieth century as a respected nation. But respect was not enough to prevent more bloodshed within its borders. When World War I began in 1914, Belgium declared its neutrality in the

Belgian cavalry and refugees evacuating Aalst in 1914

North Sea

NETHERLANDS

Passchendale
Ypres
Ghent
Brussels
BELGIUM
Artois
Liège
(German High
Command HQ)
GERMANY
Somme
FRANCE
LUXEMBOURG
Champagne
Argonne
Verdun
Paris

World War I

German advances Sept. 1914
Static Front Dec. 1914
Front Nov. 11, 1918

Slaughter in Flanders

One of the most famous poems about World War I is set in Belgium. "In Flanders Fields," by John McCrae, honors the soldiers who died fighting in Flanders. Here is the first stanza of that poem:

In Flanders fields the poppies blow
Between the crosses, row on row,
That mark our place; and in the sky
The larks, still bravely singing, fly
Scarce heard amid the guns below.

conflict. Germany, however, ignored Belgium's position and invaded the country on its way to France. Albert I, now king of Belgium, led his troops in counterattacks against the Germans and was nicknamed "the soldier king."

Some of the worst fighting of the war took place in Belgium. The city of Ypres was virtually wiped off the map, and about 80,000 Belgians died before the war ended in 1918.

Despite the losses, Belgium was not as badly damaged by the war as some other countries. The Belgians worked hard to rebuild factories and increase farm production. This process, however, was made difficult by a worldwide economic disaster, the Great Depression of the 1930s. Those tough times were soon followed by another war.

On May 10, 1940, German forces again invaded Belgium. These troops served Adolf Hitler, the head of the Nazi Party. Hitler and his Nazis wanted to take over most of Europe. After just eighteen days of fighting in Belgium, King Leopold III surrendered to the superior German forces.

Life was harsh under German occupation. Thousands of Belgians were imprisoned in a concen-

A woman and children walk through war debris as Belgium surrenders in 1940.

tration camp in Breedonk, while others were forced to work in German factories. Some Belgians supported the Nazis and even served in their military. Other Belgians were loyal to the old government and organized resistance groups to fight the Germans. Some resistance members ignored their own safety to help American and British pilots who were shot down over Belgium.

Battle in the Ardennes

U.S. and British troops drove the Germans out of Belgium in September 1944, but the war was not over for the Belgians. In late December, Germany launched its last massive counterattack. German planes bombed Antwerp and Liège. Meanwhile, in the forests of the Ardennes, German troops and tanks struck hard. This battle is known as the Battle of the Bulge because the Germans took control of a "bulge" of territory in a region controlled by the Allies. (In World War II, the *Allies* was the name given to a group of countries including the United States, Great Britain, Canada, Australia, the Soviet Union, and others. The Allies fought Germany, Italy, Japan, and their allies, who were called the *Axis*.)

The turning point of the battle came near the town of Bastogne. A small U.S. force held off the advancing Germans until reinforcements arrived. Eventually, the

The Battle of the Bulge

■ German positions Dec. 16, 1944
■ German positions Dec. 25, 1944

Allies drove the Germans out of Belgium. Today, Bastogne is the site of a memorial and museum dedicated to the soldiers who helped preserve Belgium's freedom.

Return to Prosperity

World War II ended in 1945, and the Belgians again focused on rebuilding their country. In 1951, a new king, Baudouin I, took the throne. Just twenty-one, he possessed a youthful energy that suited a nation seeking to regain its economic strength. The country once again became a center of industry and trade for Europe.

Belgium's membership in two new international organizations added to the country's status. In 1949, Belgium joined the North Atlantic Treaty Organization (NATO), a military alliance created by the United States. Brussels later became the headquarters for NATO. Then in 1958, Belgium joined the European Economic Community (EEC), now the European Union (EU). This organization promotes economic cooperation across Europe. The EEC also chose Brussels as the site of its headquarters.

In 1960, Belgium ended its colonial rule in the Congo, but it kept ties to the newly independent nation. The 1960s saw more economic growth for most Belgians. In the 1970s, however, the country faced difficult times, as did most industrialized countries around the world. Political troubles in the Middle East led to large increases in the price of oil. Belgium and other nations relied on the oil produced in the Middle East to fuel cars and factories. Belgium's economy continued to struggle during part of the 1980s. Some of these problems continued into the 1990s. But Belgium is still a major economic power, and its people enjoy a high standard of living.

NATO headquarters in Brussels

In 1993, Belgium mourned the loss of its respected king, Baudouin I. His brother Albert II then took the throne. Albert rules a land that has proven that large geographic size is not necessary to make a country great. For the Belgians, hard work and the ability to rebound from difficult times have shaped the spirit of their nation.

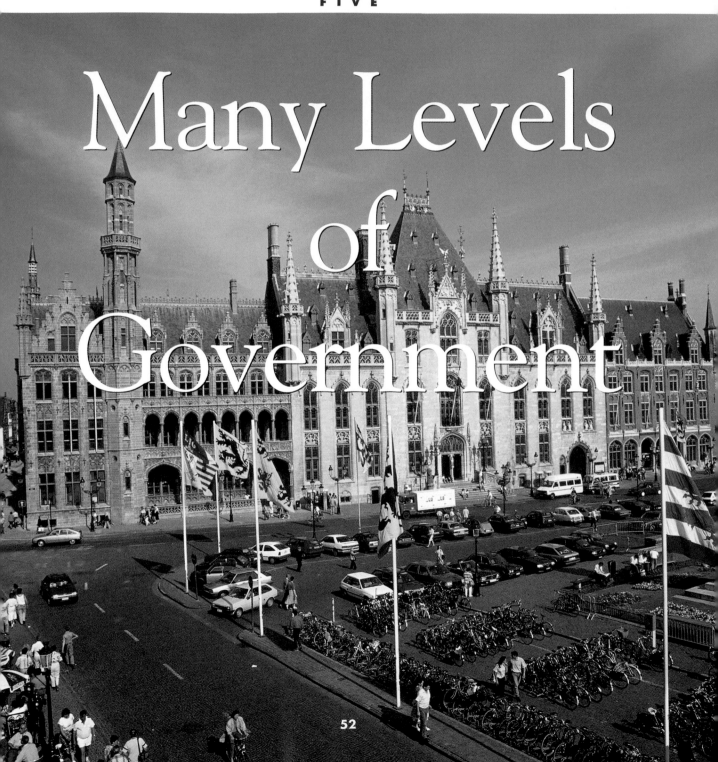

CHAPTER FIVE

Many Levels of Government

SINCE BECOMING A NATION IN 1831, BELGIUM HAS OFTEN wrestled with its cultural split. The French-speaking Walloons and the Flemish-speaking Flemings have sometimes clashed over political rights. (The country's small German-speaking population has played less of a role in this political struggle.) At times, Belgium has seemed like two nations in one. A third "mini-nation" has developed in the bilingual area around the capital of Brussels.

Along with a loyalty to their native tongue and culture, most Belgians have a fierce pride in their local communities. Those strong ties to language and local roots have often created political tensions. But the Belgians, with their skill for compromise, have been able to use democratic methods to ease the tensions.

Since 1970, Belgium has changed its Constitution four times—the last time in 1993. The aim of each change was to spread political power along cultural and geographic lines. With these changes, Belgium has created one of the most complex political systems in Europe, with five layers of

Opposite: **The Government House in Bruges**

The Parliament building

The Flag of Belgium

The Belgians adopted their flag in 1831. It features three vertical stripes of black, yellow, and red. These colors also appeared on flags waved by the Belgians in 1789, when they tried to win their independence from Austria. These same colors are found on Belgium's emblem. The emblem features one of the oldest symbols of Belgium, the *Leo Belgicus*, or Belgian lion. The lion is yellow, with red claws and tongue, and stands against a black background.

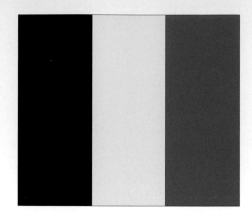

government. But the Belgians seem to welcome these layers, as they have brought the country stability. Each language group has a degree of political independence, and local communities have a large say in their own affairs. The Belgian Constitution has been called one of the strongest in the world. It has often served as a model for new countries creating their own constitutions.

A Kingdom of Sorts

Belgium's official name is the Kingdom of Belgium. The government is called a constitutional monarchy. The king is the chief of state, but he has little real power. The national government follows the rules set down in the Constitution, and the country's laws are made by the Belgian Parliament.

The king has the power to declare war and is the country's military leader during wartime. But Parliament must approve when the king declares

"La Brabanconne"

"La Brabanconne," or "The Song of Brabant," is the Belgian national anthem. Here's an English translation of the words:

Noble Belgium, forever cherished land,
To you our hearts, to you our arms.
By the pure blood shed for you, fatherland,
We swear with only one cry: you will live.
You will live, forever, large and beautiful,
And your invincible unity
Will have as an immortal motto:
King, Law, Freedom.
Will have as an immortal motto:
King, Law, Freedom
King, Law, Freedom
King, Law, Freedom

war. The king's main responsibility is to name a prime minister, a cabinet, judges, and other officials. These appointments must also be approved by Parliament.

Just as in the United States, Belgium has three national branches. The king and his cabinet make up the executive branch of the Belgian government. The cabinet is officially called the Council of Ministers. The other branches are the legislative (lawmaking) and judicial.

The prime minister is the head of Belgium's national government. Cabinet members are usually members of Parliament, and they advise the king. The king generally picks members of the most popular political parties in Belgium to serve in his cabinet.

The kingship is a hereditary position, meaning it is passed on to a relative when the reigning king dies or gives up the

Ending a Royal Crisis

After World War II, the Belgian monarchy was in trouble. King Leopold III had been criticized for his actions during the war. Some Belgians thought he had not done enough to resist Belgium's German invaders. Some Belgians demanded an end to the monarchy altogether.

In 1951, Leopold stepped down as king. His son, Baudouin, took the throne on his twenty-first birthday. During the next forty-two years, Baudouin restored the honor of the Belgian monarchy. Fluent in both French and Flemish, he helped resolve Belgium's language conflicts of the 1960s. Baudouin was seen as a warmhearted, hardworking king who had no trouble talking with his subjects. When Baudouin died suddenly in

1993, Belgians filled the streets of Brussels to mourn. An estimated half-million people visited his coffin at the royal palace.

throne. In 1991, Belgium changed its laws to allow a woman to someday take the throne, but she would still be referred to as the king, not the queen.

Belgium is a federal state. Although there is a national government, many political decisions are made by Belgium's three regions: Wallonia, Flanders, and Brussels. They have their own regional governments and pass their own laws, just as individual states do in the United States.

At the national level, Parliament passes laws relating to issues that affect the country as a whole. These include foreign policy, economic issues, and national defense. Just as in the U.S. Congress, the Belgian Parliament has two houses. The Senate has 71 members; 40 of the senators are elected directly by the voters, while the rest are chosen by provincial councils

People voting in Belgium

and other senators. The Chamber of Deputies has 150 members; all of them are elected directly by the voters. Members of both houses serve four-year terms. By law, all Belgians over the age of eighteen are required to vote in national elections, and they can be fined if they do not.

With Parliament, the prime minister works to pass laws, counting on the support of his political party and other

NATIONAL GOVERNMENT OF BELGIUM

Executive Branch

KING
(HEAD OF STATE)

PRIME MINISTER
(HEAD OF GOVERNMENT)

CABINET (MINISTERS OF STATE)

Legislative Branch (Parliament)

CHAMBER OF DEPUTIES

SENATE

Judicial Branch

SUPREME COURT OF JUSTICE
(OR CASSATION)

COURT OF APPEALS

SUPERIOR COURTS
(OR COURTS OF ASSIZE)

REGIONAL COURTS OF APPEAL

DISTRICT COURTS
(INCLUDES COMMERCE
AND LABOR TRIBUNALS)

JUSTICES OF THE PEACE
AND POLICE TRIBUNALS

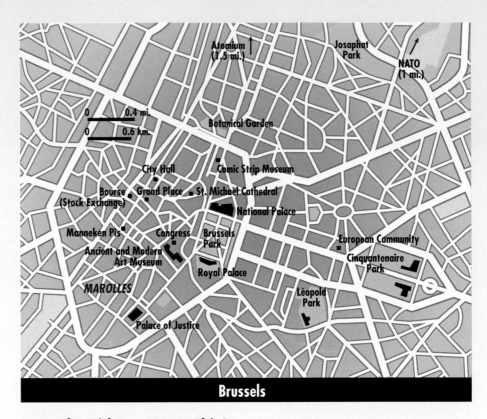

Brussels

Brussels: Did You Know This?

Brussels is the capital of Belgium, the home of its king, and the seat of many government bodies. Its buildings and streets bustle with representatives from the national, Flemish, and Brussels regional parliaments. And since the offices for the European Union are located there, Brussels is sometimes called the capital of Europe.

Year Founded: 979

Population: 950,597

About 25 percent of the population is non-Belgian. The largest immigrant groups include North Africans and Turks. About 80 percent of native Belgians in Brussels speak French and 20 percent speak Flemish.

Altitude: 50 feet (15 m) in city center; 328 feet (100 m) in outer areas

Average Daily Temperature: 37°F (3°C) in January; 64°F (18°C) in July

parties united with it. Belgium's national parties are split along linguistic lines. For example, both the Socialists and the Christian Democrats, the two major parties, have French and Flemish branches. These two parties sometimes rule together in a coalition, which means neither party has a majority of members in Parliament. The parties must join forces to pass laws. Sometimes they have to compromise on their views to reach

Prime Minister Jean-Luc Dehaene

agreements. Smaller political parties in Belgium include the Greens, who support environmental issues, and parties devoted to Flemish and Walloon cultural concerns.

In a parliamentary system such as Belgium's, the prime minister must keep the support of Parliament to stay in power. When a crisis comes, some members of Parliament might ask for a vote of no-confidence. This occurred in 1998, after Belgium's most notorious criminal escaped from prison. Prime Minister Jean-Luc Dehaene won the vote. If he had lost, a new national government would have been formed.

The Judicial Branch

The Belgian legal system is modeled on a system introduced by the French. In Belgium, the judiciary is independent from the other two branches and shares equal power with them.

Judges serve for life, meaning they are free to make their decisions without worrying about political issues of the day.

Minor offenses are tried in police courts, called tribunals, by a justice of the peace. The next level of the judiciary is the district court. These courts hear more serious criminal offenses and lawsuits brought by citizens against each other. A verdict from these courts may be appealed to one of five regional courts of appeal. District courts also include tribunals of commerce and labor.

Alleged criminals who face a sentence of five years or more have their cases heard in the Courts of Assize, or Superior Courts. Belgium has ten of these courts, and they are the only courts in the country that use a jury. The jury's verdict, however, does not have to be unanimous to convict a criminal.

Above the Superior Courts are five more Courts of Appeal. These courts review the verdicts from lower courts, to make sure the law was followed correctly. They also try government officials accused of crimes.

Belgium's highest court is the Supreme Court of Justice. At least seven judges on this court hear each case. Like the Court of Appeals, the Supreme Court of Justice decides if laws and legal procedures were properly followed. Unlike the U.S. Supreme Court, the Supreme Court of Justice cannot rule if a law is unconstitutional and must be removed from the law books. That power rests with Parliament, which takes the advice of a legal group called the Council of State.

In Belgium, anyone accused of a crime must be brought in front of a judge within twenty-four hours after being arrested.

A defendant has the legal right to have an attorney, to confront witnesses, to present evidence, and to appeal a verdict.

Regional Governments

The structure of the national parliament is repeated at the regional level. Wallonia, Flanders, and Brussels each has a prime minister and a parliament. The Walloon Parliament meets in Namur. Both the Flemish Parliament and the Brussels Parliament meet in the capital city. The regional parliaments address such issues as economics, housing, and environmental concerns.

Another layer of regional government is the language community. Three communities—Flemish, French, and German—were created in 1970. Officials on the community councils handle cultural affairs, such as arts and public broad-

City of Rebels

The citizens of Liège have a reputation for their love of political freedom. For hundreds of years bishops ruled the city. These "prince-bishops" managed to keep Liège out of the hands of neighboring kings. The people of Liège also enjoyed special protection. A law dating from the twelfth century said, "the poor man in his home is king." Its citizens prize freedom, and Liège has been called "a city of rebels."

Many Levels of Government   **61**

casting, education, and health. Together, the regional and community governments spend about 40 percent of the Belgian national budget.

Provincial and Local Government

In addition to its regions and language communities, Belgium has ten provinces. The Flemish provinces are Antwerp, East Flanders, West Flanders, Limburg, and Flemish (or North) Brabant. In Wallonia, the provinces are Hainaut, Liège, Luxembourg, Namur, and Walloon (or South) Brabant. Each province has a council with fifty to ninety members and a governor who is appointed by the king. The provincial governments handle some taxes and other affairs, but they must obey all laws passed by the national and regional parliaments.

Town Hall in Ghent was built between the fifteenth and seventeenth centuries.

Within each province are towns, also called municipalities or communes. Belgium has about 600 communes. The country has been called "a republic of communes" because of the strong attachment Belgians have to their towns and their local governments. Voters in each town elect a town council. Each council then elects a board of aldermen. This board works with the burgomaster, a political leader much like a mayor. The burgomaster is nominated by the town council and then appointed by the king. The burgomaster and the aldermen make sure all the council's actions are carried out. These politicians control fire and police departments, repair roads, and handle other local concerns.

Benelux and the European Union

Belgium also participates in political organizations that cross international borders. In 1948, Belgium joined its neighbors Luxembourg and the Netherlands in an economic agreement, the Benelux Customs Union. The name "Benelux" comes from the first letters in each country's name: **Be**lgium, **Net**herlands, **Lux**embourg. Under this agreement, the three nations act as if they are one country on some trading issues.

Ten years after the Benelux agreement, Belgium became a founding member of the European Economic Community. Today, this organization is called the European Union (EU) and has fifteen member countries. The EU promotes peace and economic growth among its members. The EU has an executive branch—the European Commission—and a parliament, but most decisions are made by the Council of Ministers, which has one minister from each member country. The ministers usually meet in Brussels. The headquarters of the EU are there as well.

The European Commission and European Parliament buildings

Trader with the World

For MUCH OF ITS HISTORY, BELGIUM HAS RELIED ON FOREIGN trade for its economic wealth. In the thirteenth century, Belgium was famous across Europe for its cloth. Six hundred years later, Belgian glass, steel, and coal were sent abroad. Today, many Belgians still earn their living making products sold around the world. The money made from these exports makes up about 60 percent of Belgium's economy. Belgium's geographic location at the crossroads of Europe helps boost its foreign trade. Belgium relies on exports more than most countries do.

The Belgians strongly support the notion of international free trade, meaning that they believe countries should not pass laws that keep out products made abroad. Belgians also

Opposite: **Cows grazing and relaxing in the fields of Dinant**

A steel factory

Belgian Money

Name: Belgian franc

Symbol: BF

A franc is made up of 100 centimes. Coins come in denominations of 50 centimes and 1, 5, 20, and 50 francs. Bills are issued in denominations of 100, 200, 500, 1,000, 2,000, 5,000, and 10,000 francs. The bills feature images of prominent Belgian people.

Starting in 2002, Belgians will jingle new coins in their pockets and pull new bills from their wallets. The European Union's Euro will replace the Belgian franc, and this new currency will be the only money used in most nations that belong to the EU.

embrace the idea of free enterprise—anyone can start a business, and the government does not own industries.

Belgians are famous for their hard work. For years, the country's industrial workers have been the most productive in Europe. It's not surprising that major U.S. manufacturers, such as Ford and General Motors, build plants in Belgium. These companies want to take advantage of the Belgians' dedication to working hard and well.

The Belgian economy, however, does have some problems. Unemployment in the late 1990s reached about 13 percent—higher than most other countries in the European Union. Also, taxes tend to be high, as the government tries to fund social programs that help the elderly, sick, and poor. These expenses are expected to rise in the twenty-first century, as Belgium's population becomes older. But even with these problems, Belgium's people enjoy a high standard of living matched in only a handful of nations.

Industry Old and New

The Industrial Revolution started in Western Europe at the beginning of the nineteenth century. Since then, Belgium has been a major industrial nation. In the nineteenth century, the coal mines and steel factories of Wallonia were among the largest in Europe. Belgium's industrial strength often seemed surprising, given the country's small size.

The Cockerill Sambre Company makes iron and steel.

Today, Belgium's coal and steel industries are in decline. They might have disappeared completely, if the government hadn't spent money to keep them alive. The country now imports many of the raw materials used in manufacturing all sorts of products. But Belgium has managed to keep jobs at companies that process metal goods and then sell them abroad. The steel industry is located primarily in Wallonia, near the cities of Charleroi and Liège.

Like most other older industrial nations, Belgium has turned away from "dirty" industries such as coal and steel and toward more high-tech manufacturing. Flanders has benefited most from this high-tech boom. After World War II, land in that region was cheap, so companies built modern factories there. Flanders also had a large pool of workers looking for jobs. Today, Flanders produces more than half of Belgium's total economic output.

The most important industrial products manufactured in Belgium today include chemicals, prescription drugs, electronic equipment, autos, and plastics. Belgium is a leader in making the special dyes and chemicals used in photography. Other major industries are refining petroleum and processing food. Smaller, but growing, high-tech industries include the manufacture of robots, lasers, and biotechnology products. Flanders is among the top three high-tech regions in Europe.

Workers restore ancient tapestries at the Chaudoir Factory.

Three of Belgium's oldest products are also among its most valuable: glass, textiles, and diamonds. The Belgian glass industry began in the Middle Ages. Today, light pours into office buildings in Singapore through window glass made in Belgium, and many European drivers look through Belgian windshields. Belgium leads Europe in the production of many types of industrial glass.

Plastic Man

In the early twentieth century, Leo Hendrik Baekeland was one of the pioneers of plastic. Baekeland was born outside Ghent in 1863. At thirteen, he began working for a shoemaker, but he left that trade to study science at the University of Ghent. Baekeland taught chemistry there and in Bruges before leaving for the United States in 1889.

In the United States, Baekeland developed a new kind of photographic paper. He made a fortune when he sold his invention to the Eastman Kodak camera company. Baekeland continued to experiment with different chemicals, and in 1907 he created the first synthetic plastic—Bakelite. This material could be molded into different shapes and then hardened. Bakelite products included billiard balls, toilet seats, radios, and jewelry. Today, some items made out of Bakelite are valued by collectors in the United States.

The textile industry has declined from its glory years when Bruges and Ghent were leading cloth centers, but it remains an important part of the Belgian economy. Almost all its raw materials come from abroad. Belgium's textile factories produce lace, carpets, and fabrics for homes and industries. Carpets are Belgium's major textile product, making up about 40 percent of the industry's total production.

Fashion Statement

In the world of fashion, designers in Paris, New York, and London set most trends. But since the 1980s, Antwerp has also become a fashion center, thanks to the work of the Antwerp Six. This group of Belgian designers first displayed their clothes together at a 1986 fashion show in London. Their work brought attention to the fashion industry in Antwerp. The city's Academy of Arts has a fashion department that trains clothing designers.

The Antwerp Six—who now number seven—includes Martin Margiela, Dirk Bikkembergs, and Ann Demeulemeester, who is called Ann D. by her fans. Although their individual styles vary, in general the Antwerp Six favor simple, smart clothes, such as Ann D.'s stylish black suit. The success of the Antwerp Six has attracted other designers to Antwerp, and Belgian fashions are now known around the world.

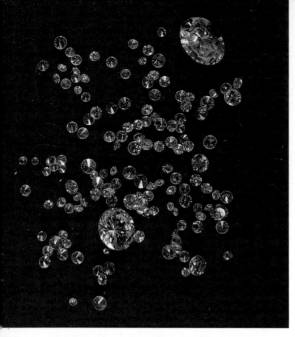

A display of cut diamonds

While glass and fabric are common items, diamonds are one of the world's rarest goods. Antwerp first became a diamond center in the fifteenth century, and today it is the diamond capital of the world. The glittering stones come to Belgium from diamond mines around the world before being shipped to their final destination. Many diamonds are cut in Antwerp before being sold as jewelry. Some of these cut diamonds are also used in industry.

What Belgium Grows, Makes, and Mines	
Agriculture	
Sugar beets	6,081,000 tons
Potatoes	2,308,000 tons
Wheat	1,453,000 tons
Manufacturing *(value added in U.S.$)*	
Chemicals	4,771,000,000
Transport equipment	3,632,000,000
Textiles	2,056,000,000
Mining	
Quartz	500,000 metric tons
Barite	30,000 metric tons
Granite	2,105,000 cubic meters

Strength in Service

The largest sector of the Belgian economy is the service industry. About 70 percent of all Belgian workers have service jobs. The service industry includes banking, insurance, tourism, education, sales, and public service. The largest sector of the service economy is government work.

Because so many Belgians speak more than one language, they are desirable employees for large international companies. Many foreign corporations have offices in Belgium, especially in Brussels.

Belgians also travel the world to share their expertise with other nations. Belgian engineers and consultants are world leaders in such fields as electrical power, construction, and food processing.

Tourism is an important part of the service industry.

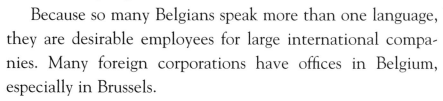

A young girl helping out on a farm

Working the Land and Water

Although Belgium has an industrialized economy, about 46 percent of its land is still used for farming and raising livestock. But thanks to modern farming methods, only about 3 percent of the country's workers are needed to harvest crops and raise farm animals. Belgium's farmers are able to grow about 80 percent of the country's food needs.

Resources

▨	Industrial		Cereals, Dairy
■	Dairy		Forests
□	Cash Crops	C	Coal

The most important agricultural activity in Belgium is raising livestock. Each year, Belgian farmers raise more than 3 million head of cattle and about 7 million hogs. These numbers tend to grow slightly each year. The Belgian diet features a lot of meat and dairy products. The native livestock provide all the country's meat, and Belgian dairy cattle provide all the milk and butter Belgians need.

Horticulture, or the growing of plants and trees, is also an important part of Belgium's agriculture. Belgium is a world leader in exporting begonias and azaleas, two popular garden plants.

Food crops make up the smallest percentage of Belgium's agriculture. The most fertile farmlands are found in the provinces of East and West Flanders and Flemish and Walloon Brabant. The number of farms in Belgium has shrunk over the years, while existing farms have increased in size. Overall, however, the amount of land used to grow crops is falling. About 50 percent of Belgium's farmland is used for pastures, and another 25 percent is used to raise grains. Belgium's top grain is wheat, but corn, barley, and other grains are also grown.

The leading vegetable crops are sugar beets and potatoes. Belgian farmers also grow such fruit as apples, cherries, and pears. Very few fruits and vegetables are sold in other countries. One exception is chicory, also called Belgian endive. This leafy vegetable is used in salads or eaten on its own.

Fishing is only a small part of the Belgian economy. Most of the commercial fishing is done in the North Sea. Belgium's fishers catch about 30,000 tons of fish a year.

Forests and Mines

About 20 percent of Belgium's land is covered with forests, but the country has a tiny forestry industry. About 25,000 Belgians work in the wood-processing industry, which includes furniture making. Belgium imports much of the wood used for local woodworking.

Since many of Belgium's largest coal mines have closed, mining plays only a small part in the Belgian economy. Some coal is still mined in Kempenland. This coal is used mostly in the steel industry. Other products mined are sand and gravel, which are used mostly to make cement. Small amounts of marble and limestone are taken from Belgian quarries.

Belgium's railways are an important means of transportation.

Power and Transportation

To keep its economy growing, Belgium relies on its energy and transportation systems. About 60 percent of Belgium's energy comes from nuclear power. Almost all of the rest comes from plants that burn coal and oil. In recent years, some environmental groups have expressed concern about the risks of nuclear power.

Belgium's transportation system features one of the best railways in the world.

Antwerp is Belgium's largest seaport.

The government operates slightly more than 2,300 miles (3,701 km) of track. Passengers can reach many major European cities by high-speed trains. Belgian roads and highways cover about 85,000 miles (136,790 km).

For water transportation, Belgian and international ships use the country's 900 miles (1,448 km) of canals. At 80 miles (129 km), the Albert Canal is the longest. It links Liège with Antwerp. Belgium's major seaports include Antwerp, Ghent, and Zeebrugge. Brussels and Liège, among other cities, receive inland ship traffic at their river ports. Liège is the third-largest river port in Europe.

Belgium's international airport is located just outside Brussels. Sabena, the national airline, has flights from the airport to cities around the world. Antwerp also has a smaller airport that offers flights to many parts of Europe.

News and Views

Belgium's newspapers, radio stations, and TV channels have both French and Flemish versions. The country has radio and TV stations owned by the government, as well as privately owned TV stations. Cable networks bring in programming from France, England, Germany, Italy, the United States, and the Netherlands.

Belgium has about thirty daily newspapers. The largest are published in Brussels, including the Flemish papers *Het Nieuwsblad* and *Het Laatse Nieuws*, and the French papers

Le Soir and *La Dernière Heure*. The country also has about 500 weekly papers and 8,000 weekly and monthly magazines. Many Belgians are turning to the Internet to receive the latest local and international news.

Belgium's Workers

Belgium's economy depends on almost 4 million workers to keep it going. Many Belgians belong to unions, which try to guarantee their members good wages and benefits. Most Belgians work a forty-hour week and receive four weeks of paid vacation each year.

Belgians pay some of the highest taxes in Europe, and they are known for trying to find ways to avoid paying these high rates. Surveys say half of all Belgians evade paying some taxes. Many people put their money in foreign banks. Some families have been known to set up small companies with relatives as the only employees. They hope to reduce their taxes by deducting family expenses as business costs. In some cases, however, the Belgian government deliberately lowers taxes for some companies. These companies get tax breaks if they invest in new plants or improve existing ones.

Despite their high taxes, Belgians still find ways to save money. They have one of the highest saving rates in Europe.

A newsstand in Brussels displays the French-language newspaper *Le Soir.*

A Land of Three Peoples

BELGIUM IS ONE OF THE MOST DENSELY POPULATED countries in the world. In each square mile lives an average of 864 people (334 per sq km). Most of those people are either Walloons or Flemings. Ever since Belgium became an independent nation in 1831, it has tried to address the needs of those two distinct peoples.

The linguistic differences of the Walloons and the Flemings have sometimes created political and social problems in Belgium. But rather than break their country into two nations or seek union with a neighboring country, the Belgians have found ways to keep all their people content under one national banner.

Population distribution in Belgium

The People and Languages of Belgium

Population

Fleming	55%
Walloon	33%
Mixed or other ethnic group	12%

Language

Flemish	56%
French	32%
Bilingual	11%
German	1%

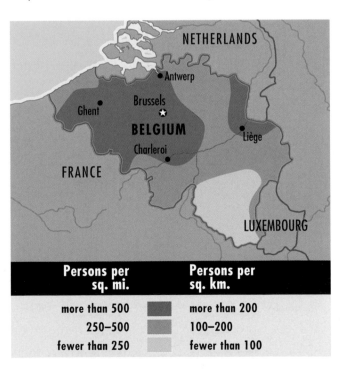

Persons per sq. mi.		Persons per sq. km.
more than 500		more than 200
250–500		100–200
fewer than 250		fewer than 100

Flemish schoolgirls in the city of Antwerp

The Flemings

The Flemings make up more than half of Belgium's population. About 6 million people live in Flanders. The native people of Flanders have ties to the Franks, the Germanic people who came to Belgium more than 1,700 years ago. Of course, over the centuries, other people from inside and outside Europe have settled in Flanders.

Most of today's Flemings speak Flemish. Some people compare the differences between Flemish and the Dutch spoken in the Netherlands to the differences between the English spoken in North America and Great Britain.

For many centuries, French was the language spoken by Belgium's foreign rulers. The wealthiest people spoke French. Some Flemings felt like second-class citizens because of their language. But soon after Belgium gained its independence, the Flemings began a struggle to give their language equal status with French. Authors and politicians led this battle, which resulted in Flemish becoming an official language in 1898.

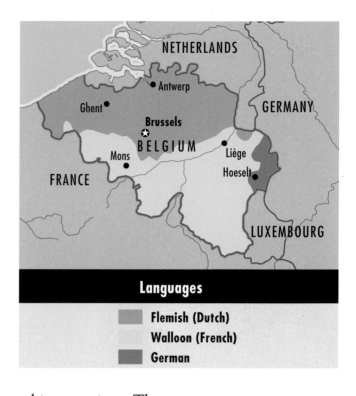

But that did not end the language battles. In the 1960s, some Flemings resented the use of French in Flanders. They began to protest. In some cases, they interrupted church services that were held in French. Protests also broke out at the University of Leuven (Louvain) in Flanders. The school had a French-speaking section. The Flemish protestors wanted to move this section to a new university in Wallonia, but the French students and teachers wanted to stay in Louvain. The Belgian government was able to end the protests without any major violence. Constitutional changes in 1970 created new communities in Belgium based on language.

Today, the Flemings are in the majority. They also have a stronger economy than the French-speaking Walloons have. Most Flemings no longer feel inferior to the Walloons or struggle against them. But a small number of Flemings want to make themselves as distinct from the Walloons as possible. They would like to make Flanders a separate nation from Belgium.

In Praise of the Flemings

In the 1830s, author Hendrik Conscience wanted to stir the Flemings' pride in their language and history. He wrote a number of books in Flemish that looked at the best moments in Flanders's past. His most famous work was *The Lion of Flanders*, about the Battle of the Golden Spurs, a 1302 Flemish victory over French forces.

In his foreword to *The Lion of Flanders*, Conscience used strong words to express his feelings. He said the government was trying to turn the Flemings into Walloons and called this act "despicable." He told the reader, "You are a Fleming and shall remain a Fleming. And so this glorious name will live till the end of the world..."

Conscience's works were so popular with the Flemings that he was sometimes called the Flemish author who taught his people how to read.

The Walloons

The French-speaking Walloons make up a little more than 30 percent of Belgium's population. Their ethnic roots go back to the Celtic tribes that lived in Belgium before the Roman invasions of the first century B.C.

For many centuries, the Walloons felt they had more in common with France and the French than with the Flemings to the north. Many Walloons also felt superior to the Flemings

A Walloon family in Mons

Flemish and French Pronunciation Key

For most English speakers, Flemish vowel sounds can be hard to pronounce.
Here's a sample of some of those sounds:

Letter(s)	Pronounce as	Example	Pronunciation
au	ow (as in "cow")	kabeljauw	cabbleyow
ee	ai (as in "hail")	een	ain
eie	ay (as in "say")	Leie	lay
ieu	ee-oo	nieuw	nee-oo
ou	ou (as in "out")	zout	zout

Here are some of the vowel sounds found in French:

Letter(s)	Pronounce as	Example	Pronunciation
a	ah (as in "father")	classe	klahs
a	a (as in "cat")	balle	bal
é	ay (as in "hate")	café	ka-FAY
è	e (as in "there")	sévère	say-VEHR
i	ee (as in "feet")	ici	ee-CEE
o	u (as in "but")	poste	pust
ou	oo (as in "boot")	route	root

Common Expressions in Flemish and French

English	Flemish	French
yes	ja	oui
no	nee	non
please	alstublieft	s'il vous plaît
thank you	dank u	merci
hello (good day)	goedendag	bonjour
good evening	goedenavond	bonsoir
good-bye	tot ziens	au revoir
How are you?	Hoe maakt u het?	Comment allez-vous?
very well	goed	très bien
How much?	Hoeveel?	Combien?
Where is . . . ?	Waar is . . . ?	Où est . . . ?

Les Marolles

In a tiny corner of Brussels, near the Palais de Justice, is Les Marolles. The people of this neighborhood speak their own dialect, one that was developed hundreds of years ago. At the time, Flemings and Walloons lived side-by-side on crowded streets, and Spanish soldiers of King Philip II patrolled the area too. The language that developed here—Marolliens—is mostly French, with Flemish and Spanish expressions mixed in.

Over time, Les Marolles shrunk, as homes and businesses were torn down to make way for new buildings. Today, perhaps only 10,000 people live in Les Marolles. Many of them are poor immigrants, and few citizens of Brussels still speak the neighborhood's unique dialect. Les Marolles is perhaps best known for the huge flea market held every morning at the Place du Jeu de Balle.

because they spoke an international language used by royalty and prominent people. And after 1830, Wallonia had a much stronger economy than Flanders did.

Today, however, the Walloons face some economic struggles. Their traditional sources of wealth—coal mining and steelmaking—have declined. The Walloons have also seen the Flemings become a majority of the population. But the Walloons have linguistic protection in their region, and French is still the favored language in Brussels. Although the city is officially bilingual (French and Flemish), about 80 percent of the residents in the capital region speak French.

The Germans

Belgium's German community lives in a small strip of land between the German border and the city of Liège. About 70,000 German-speaking people live there. Many of them work across the border in Germany. Students in this region are required to study French when they enter first grade and a third language as they grow older.

The German-speaking Belgians have not protested or used politics to gain rights for their community. But they have received many of the social and political privileges the Flemings and the Walloons have. Since 1963, German has been Belgium's third official language.

The German region of Belgium was added to the country after World War I. During World War II, the area was controlled by Nazi Germany. It returned to Belgian rule in 1944. Many of the German-speaking Belgians were later suspected of being traitors during the war. Today, however, the people of the region consider themselves loyal Belgians who just happen to speak German as their native language.

Other Belgians

Just under 1 million people who live in Belgium are from foreign countries. More than half of them come from other European Union nations. About 40 percent of these foreign-born residents come from Italy. In the 1950s, Italians came to work in Belgium's coal mines, and their numbers increased during the 1960s, when Belgium's economy grew. Some of these Italians and other immigrants have become Belgian citizens, while many work in the country for the EU, NATO, or international corporations. Since the end of communism in Russia and Eastern Europe, more people from that region have also settled in Belgium.

People of all backgrounds and nationalities live in Belgium.

There are programs to help keep children off the streets. Here, the boys are learning to create and perform music.

Population of Major Cities

Metro Brussels	950,597
Antwerp	453,030
Ghent	225,469
Charleroi	204,899
Liège	189,510
Bruges	115,500

Another large group of immigrants comes from North Africa, particularly Morocco, and Turkey. Many of the Middle Eastern and African immigrants live in Brussels. In some districts of the city, as much as 50 percent of the population was born in a foreign country.

Many of the more recent immigrants are Muslims. They tend to have darker skin than native Belgians. Their different ethnic and religious backgrounds sometimes make these immigrants the targets of racism, especially during bad economic times. They tend to lose their jobs first when companies have to get rid of workers. Then they are forced to rely on the government for social services. Some Belgians dislike spending tax money on people they think of as foreigners. But racial violence is rare in Belgium, and in Brussels thousands of people have gathered for rallies promoting racial tolerance.

Where and How People Live

Across Belgium, most people live in or near urban areas. Belgium is one of the most urbanized countries in Europe. About 30 percent of the population live in the country's five largest cities. The Ardennes is the least populated area of Belgium.

As is typical in most modern industrialized nations, Belgium offers its citizens excellent health care and education. Public health insurance pays almost 95 percent of all medical bills. The country has 36 doctors for every 10,000 people and about 400 hospitals. The typical Belgian can expect to live 77 years, slightly longer than the average American does.

Schooling is free in Belgium for children between the ages of six and eighteen, and all students are required to attend during those years. Belgium has eight major national universities. Almost the entire adult population is able to read and write.

Students enjoying classroom activities at Homborch School in Brussels

Beliefs

FOR CENTURIES, ALMOST EVERY BELGIAN BELONGED TO THE Roman Catholic Church. Today, the country's royal family is the only Catholic royal family in northern Europe. But for many Belgians, the Catholic Church no longer plays an important role in their daily lives.

Under the Belgian constitution, Belgians are allowed to worship any way they choose. Some follow no religion at all. By law, the government cannot ask people what church they belong to, so membership numbers are not totally accurate.

Opposite: **Saint Gertrude Abbey**

Intricate statues adorn the exterior of Saint Paul's Church.

Major Religions of Belgium

Roman Catholic	75%
Muslim	2.5%
Protestant	1%
Other (Jewish, freethinking, nonpracticing)	21.5%

Belgium has four major religions: Catholicism, Protestantism, Islam, and Judaism. The government helps pay the salary of the religious leaders of these four faiths.

The Roots of Catholicism

When the Frankish king Clovis ruled what is now Belgium, there was only one Christian faith. This religion was the root of modern Roman Catholicism and the faith that has shaped Belgian culture. Even before Clovis converted to Christianity, Belgium had a Christian region, called a see, controlled by a bishop based in Tongeren.

A Saintly Founder

The city of Mons, in the province of Hainaut, had its roots in religion. In the seventh century, Saint Waudru founded a convent (right) located in what became the center of Mons. The daughter of a count of Hainaut, Waudru married a nobleman and had a family. But as she grew older, she decided to devote herself to her faith.

After her husband entered an abbey, Waudru began to live a simple life. Seeking even more time for prayer, she started a convent, later called Chateaulieu. Saint Waudru was given credit for miraculously healing the sick, both during and after her life. Bones said to be from the saint are kept in Mons and paraded through the city once a year. Saint Waudru's four children, who shared her strong faith, were also named saints by the Catholic Church.

A Leading Lady

The largest Gothic church in Belgium is Antwerp's Onze Lieve Vrouwekathedral (Cathedral of Our Lady). Begun in 1352, the church took almost 200 years to finish. It features a tower about 400 feet (122 m) tall, the only one of five planned towers actually built. Inside the tower are forty-seven bells. On Monday evenings during the summer, the bells play tunes for people who gather outside the church. The Cathedral of Our Lady also has an onion-shaped dome in the middle, seven aisles, and 125 stone pillars.

Over the centuries, the church has survived a fire, an attack by angry Protestants, and occupation by French troops. Despite this, the church still has impressive wood carvings, stained glass, and other valuable art, including three pieces by Peter Paul Rubens, one of Belgium's greatest painters.

During the centuries after Clovis, Christianity spread across Belgium. Irish monks and French priests helped bring this new faith to the Belgians, who began building monasteries and churches. By the time of Charlemagne, in the early ninth century, Wallonia had twenty-two large monasteries and Flanders had three.

At this time, and for centuries to come, Christianity influenced all parts of life for most Europeans. Monks and priests were usually the best-educated people in a community. Church leaders were often united with local rulers. Church rituals and festivals provided a social life for the average citizens.

Churches themselves were the most magnificent buildings in Belgium. The first churches were built in a style called Romanesque. They had thick walls and small windows. But a later style, called Gothic, enabled builders to erect churches with huge towers, called spires, and massive windows. The greatest churches in Belgium are Gothic, and most were built between the twelfth and fifteenth centuries.

National Religious Holidays

Easter Monday	Day after Easter
Ascension Day	Sixth Thursday after Easter
Whit Monday	Seventh Monday after Easter
Assumption Day	August 15
All Saints' Day	November 1
Christmas	December 25

Martin Luther preaching to the Protestants

In 1517, Christianity began to split into factions. Some religious thinkers, led by Martin Luther, challenged traditional beliefs and the role of priests and bishops. Various Protestant groups inspired by Luther broke away from the Roman Catholic Church. These religious disagreements led to political battles across Europe, and Belgium was caught in the middle.

The new Protestant religions gained strength all around Belgium. The Netherlands, to the north, was founded as a Protestant nation. But Belgium kept the traditional faith and has remained largely Roman Catholic ever since.

Belgium's Famous Churches and Cathedrals

City	Church	Date
Antwerp	Cathedral of Our Lady	14th–16th centuries
Bruges	Church of Our Lady	13th–15th centuries
Brussels	Cathedral of Saint Michael	13th century
Ghent	Saint Bavo's	14th–15th centuries
Liège	Cathedral of Saint Paul	10th century
Mons	Collegiate Church of St. Waudru	15th century
Tournai	Cathedral of Our Lady	12th century

Monasteries, Convents, and Abbeys

Throughout Belgium's history, monasteries, convents, and abbeys have played an important role in religious and daily life. The monks and nuns who resided in these communities chose to live apart from society to show their faith to God. Yet they also had some contact with the people who lived in the towns and villages around them.

Monasteries, convents, and abbeys are run by groups called religious orders. Many of these orders have lost members over the years. They have sold their land and closed their buildings. But during the Middle Ages, these religious orders were among the wealthiest landowners in Belgium. With their wealth, monasteries were able to help the poor.

The courtyard of an ancient abbey

The Cistercians were one of Belgium's largest religious orders. Cistercian monks took a vow of silence and spoke only when necessary. They believed in hard work and were well known for their farming techniques. One branch of the Cistercians, the Trappists, are still active in Belgium. They are renowned for their fine beer-making skills.

Religious women often joined convents, where they devoted their life to the church and performed charity. But some women who did not want to spend their whole lives as nuns lived in special convents called *begijnhofs*. The first of these convents were said to have started during the Crusades, when European soldiers went to fight in Jerusalem. The widows of these soldiers needed security and companionship, so they went to live in the begijnhofs. The women spent their time making lace, cooking, and taking care of the sick. A few begijnhofs remain in Belgium, though the residents today are mostly nuns.

Missionaries and Pilgrims

The deep faith of some Belgian Catholics has led them to do missionary work for the church. This work involves trying to convert others, usually poor people, to Catholicism. In the sixteenth century, Belgian priests traveled with the Spanish to the New World. Later, some Belgian missionaries worked with the French in Quebec, Canada. One of them was Louis Hennepin. He won fame as the first European to explore the upper portion of the Mississippi River.

In the nineteenth century, Belgium had its own colony in central Africa. Belgian missionaries traveled to the Congo and baptized the people as Catholics. Today, Belgian priests still work in some central African nations.

Belgians have also traveled within their own country for religious purposes. Belgium is the site of a few Catholic shrines, holy places where some people believe miracles occurred. One of these is the Basilica of Our Lady, in Halle.

Priest to the Sick

Belgium's most beloved missionary was Father Damien. Born Joseph de Veuster in 1840, Damien grew up in Tremelo. At twenty, he took his religious vows, and he was ordained four years later, while already working in Hawaii. At this time, Hawaii was an independent nation. In 1873, Father Damien arrived on the island of Molokai, where he began the work that made him famous.

On Molokai was a colony for people with Hansen's disease, also called leprosy. Leprosy causes large bumps on the body and can damage the eyes and nose. In Damien's time there was no cure for the disease, and because it spread easily, people with leprosy were forced to live off by themselves. Father Damien showed compassion to people with the disease and tried to improve their living conditions at the remote colony. After sixteen years on Molokai, Father Damien died of leprosy.

In 1936, Father Damien's body was returned to Belgium and laid to rest at Sint Antonius Kapel in Louvain. In 1994, the Belgian priest was beatified by Pope John Paul II—the final step before making Damien a Roman Catholic saint.

The wooden statue of Mary in the Basilica of Our Lady in Halle is said to have miraculous powers.

This church features a wooden statue of Mary, the mother of Jesus Christ, that is supposed to have miraculous powers. Devout Catholics called pilgrims march through Halle to the church every year to see this statue.

Another holy place is in Saint Hubert, in the Ardennes. According to local legend, an eighth-century Belgian hunter named Hubert saw an image of a cross between the antlers of a stag. A voice then told Hubert to become a missionary. Hubert later became Saint Hubert, and today hunters travel to the town named after him.

Belgian Catholics Today

Although most Belgians still call themselves Catholics, the religion has lost some influence in daily life. Traditionally, Walloon Catholics were said to be more devout than the Catholics of Flanders, but that is becoming less true. Catholics in both regions seem to regularly attend Mass less often than in the past and may not strictly follow all the church's teachings. But many parents still send their children to Catholic schools, and Belgium's ties to its Catholic roots still exist. The Catholic Church places importance on the family and its unity, and most Belgians still feel strong family ties. And many festivals that began as Catholic celebrations are still a large part of Belgium's cultural life.

Some of these festivals include pre-Lenten celebrations, much like the French Mardi Gras. The festivities in the town of Binche start about a month before Lent, the solemn forty days before Easter. The events are topped off with public dancing that goes nonstop for twenty-four hours.

In Brussels, the Ommegang festival is held each July. This celebration marks the anniversary of the arrival of a statue of Mary in the city in the fourteenth century. Today's celebration, however, puts more emphasis on colorful costumes than on religious devotion.

The colorful costumes and flags of the Ommegang festival

Saint Nicholas Day

One special day celebrated throughout Belgium is Saint Nicholas Day (December 6). Although not an official religious holiday, Saint Nicholas Day is more important for Belgian children than Christmas. This is the day when the children receive presents.

Legends say Saint Nicholas rides to Belgian homes on a donkey. Children leave food for him and carrots for his donkey. The children also leave their shoes or slippers by the chimney so Saint Nicholas can fill them with gifts. The American figure of Santa Claus is based on Saint Nicholas. The real Saint Nicholas lived in the fourth century and was a bishop in what is now Turkey.

Other Faiths

The largest mosque in Brussels

About 100,000 Belgians belong to a variety of Protestant faiths. Some belong to the Lutheran church—the church that follows the teachings of Martin Luther. Others are Anglicans. They follow a faith based in England. Other sects with Protestant roots serve an even smaller number of Belgians.

The largest non-Catholic religion in Belgium is Islam, whose followers are called Muslims. The country has about 250,000 Muslims. Most of them are immigrants from North Africa and Turkey, and their descendants. Muslim churches are called mosques, and Belgium's largest one is in Brussels.

Belgium has about 35,000 Jews. Most live in Antwerp and Brussels. During World War II, many Belgian Jews were sent to German concentration camps. Some went voluntarily, thinking the camps offered better living conditions than in Belgium, which was occupied by the Germans. Later, the Germans forced the Jews to go to the camps. About 25,000 Belgian Jews died in concentration camps. Some Jewish children managed to escape the camps by living with Belgian families that were not Jewish. The pain of being separated from their parents and denying their Jewish faith haunted many of them for years.

Freethinkers

During the eighteenth and nineteenth centuries, many Europeans began to turn away from organized Catholic and Protestant churches. Some joined so-called free churches. Others gave up on religion altogether. Today these people are collectively called freethinkers, and they make up about 12 percent of Belgium's population. One of the largest groups of freethinkers is the Freemasons.

In recent years, some freethinkers have adopted ceremonies and institutions similar to ones used by Catholics. This movement is called "laicity." Some members of the laicity movement have asked the government to officially recognize it as a religion, just as it does the major faiths.

CHAPTER

NINE

Time for the Mind and Body

98

B ELGIUM'S ROLE AS A COMMERCIAL CENTER OF EUROPE has also made it a center for art. In the past, wealthy merchants and noble families could afford to hire expert painters and sculptors and build lavish buildings. The Roman Catholic Church also contributed to this cultural creativity. Belgium's grandest churches are not merely houses of worship. They serve as "living museums" with beautiful art designed to inspire the faithful.

Today, Belgians are understandably proud of the many artistic masters who lived and worked in their country. And in modern times, Belgium has continued to produce talented artists in all fields.

Belgians, like many other people around the world, also fill their leisure time with physical activities. Sports—both watching and playing them—are a favorite national pastime.

Flemish Art

During the fifteenth century, artists across Europe were developing new styles and painting new subjects. This was the time of the Renaissance,

Opposite: **The National Maritime Museum in Antwerp**

Teenagers playing basketball near the European Union headquarters

The Betrothal of the Arnolfini by Jan van Eyck

a "rebirth" of classical ideas of beauty. Although the Renaissance is often associated with the wealthy city-states of Italy, a Northern Renaissance took place as well. This explosion of art was centered in Flanders and the Netherlands. A Flemish school of art developed, and Flanders continued to produce great painters through the seventeenth century.

One of the first Flemish masters was Jan van Eyck. Along with his brother Hubert, van Eyck painted religious scenes on wood. The brothers spent much of their career in Bruges and developed new techniques for working with oil-based paints. Their Ghent Altarpiece, located in Ghent's St. Bavo's Cathedral, is a masterpiece of fifteenth-century religious art. Jan van Eyck is also famous for his work *The Betrothal of the Arnolfini*. Painted in 1434, this piece introduced a new level of detail in art. Its subject was the wealthy businessman who had hired van Eyck to paint his and his bride's portrait. The painting marked the beginning of a trend away from religious subjects in paintings.

Working around the same time as Jan van Eyck was Robert Campin, also called the Master of Flemalle. He was the teacher of another famous Flemish painter, Rogier van der Weyden. Van der Weyden in turn instructed Hans Memling. Working out of Bruges, Memling was the most popular Flemish painter in the last half of the fifteenth century.

Portrait of a Lady by Rogier van der Weyden

Sixteenth-Century Masters

In the late fifteenth century, Flanders produced one of the most unusual artists in history, Hieronymus Bosch. A devout Catholic, Bosch painted many works with religious themes, but they were crammed with images of gruesome creatures and humans suffering for their sins. In ways, Bosch was ahead of his time. He has been called the first surrealist painter. The term "surrealist" was first used to describe art in the twentieth century. Surrealist art draws on dreams and nonrealistic images.

A more traditional Flemish master of the time was Pieter Bruegel. He was known as Bruegel the Elder, because his son

The Peasant Wedding by
Pieter Bruegel the Elder

Pieter was also a successful painter. Bruegel the Elder typically
painted detailed scenes of peasants. Such works as *The Peasant
Wedding* offer historians insight into how Flemings lived during the sixteenth century. Pieter Bruegel the Younger painted
similar scenes of everyday life. But he also had a touch of
Bosch's dark view of human nature and was nicknamed Hell
Bruegel. Bruegel the Elder had another son, Jan, who also
painted. He was sometimes called Velvet Bruegel, because
he liked to paint detailed pictures of flowers placed against
velvet backgrounds.

The last great Flemish painter of the era was Peter Paul Rubens. He was born in Germany to Belgian parents and educated in Italy. Rubens then settled in Belgium. In 1609, he became the court painter for the ruling Hapsburgs. Rubens painted altarpieces, lavish paintings, and small portraits. His works often showed people and animals in motion, and he was famous for capturing the well-rounded Flemish women of his day. The word "Rubenesque" is sometimes used today to describe similar women. A small museum dedicated to Rubens sits on the site of his house in Antwerp.

Although best known as an oil painter, Rubens once worked on tapestry design. During the fifteenth and sixteenth centuries, many Flemish artists used their talents to design tapestries. After a design was drawn, five or six workers used colored threads to weave the design. Sometimes threads made from gold and silver were also used. Belgian tapestries were hung in palaces and churches across Europe.

Into the Modern Era

After Rubens, Flemish painting lost its influence in Europe as painters from France and other countries gained prominence. While Belgian painters still made fine works of art, the country had few great masters. In the nineteenth century, François Joseph Navez was known for his scenes from history and ancient mythology. Another Belgian painter of the time was Antoine Joseph Wiertz, who painted on huge canvases up to 30 feet (9 m) tall.

In more recent times, three Belgians artists stand out. James Ensor began painting in the nineteenth century, but he won his reputation in the twentieth. His best-known work, *The Entry of Christ into Brussels*, features strong colors and chaotic action. René Magritte was a surrealist famous for his dreamlike scenes. In one Magritte painting, a train roars out of a fireplace. In another, men in long dark coats fall from the

The Sorcerer by René Magritte

Museum for the Ages

Brussels's Cinquantenaire Park was built in 1880 to celebrate the fiftieth anniversary of Belgian independence. The park features ornate buildings now used as museums. The grandest of these is the Cinquantenaire Museum (formerly called the Royal Museums of Art and History). This sprawling museum has art objects dating back to ancient Egypt, Greece, and Rome. One of the museum's most famous collections is in the Treasure Room. The room holds medieval jewelry and other rare items. Only fifty visitors can enter the room at one time.

sky like rain. Paul Delvaux was another Belgian surrealist. In his work, Delvaux often showed skeletons and living people in the middle of eerie landscapes.

One modern Belgian artist who won recognition as both a painter and a sculptor is Rik Wouters. He worked during the early twentieth century. Wouters's paintings, which feature vibrant colors, were part of a movement called fauvism. Wouters often used his wife, Nel, as his model for his paintings and sculptures.

Belgium's great artworks from the past and present are displayed in a number of museums, as well as in galleries and churches. Brussels has the Museum of Ancient Art and Museum of Modern Art, two connected buildings filled with art treasures from around the world. Both Antwerp and Bruges feature museums with works by many Flemish masters. Liège, Charleroi, and other cities have museums as well.

Ancient Craft in Modern Times

Dainty white lace has been a fashion favorite in Europe for more than 400 years. Belgium has always been a center for lace making. The more expensive pieces featured images woven into the cloth. Today, the lace makers in and around Brussels are still famous for their product. Working by hand, they use methods that are centuries old. Lace making is slow, hard work, and fewer Belgians are learning this delicate craft today. But Brussels has a museum dedicated to lace, and the Cinquantenaire Museum has a large collection of fine lace.

Buildings with Style

Belgium has fine examples of architecture from many periods. Many of its churches date back more than 1,000 years, when the Romanesque style was popular. Gothic architecture, introduced from France, is also seen throughout Belgium.

Belgium's cities are known for their well-preserved buildings. Bruges is the most famous of these. Its city center looks almost exactly as it did 400 years ago. The Grand Place in Brussels is also admired for its beauty. This marketplace is not

The daily flower market at the Grand Place in Brussels

The interior of a house that Victor Horta built for himself in 1898

as old as the market areas in other Belgian cities. Some of the buildings that line the square feature columns and statues and are decorated with gold.

Brussels is also the home to many more modern buildings. In the late nineteenth century, the Belgian architect Victor Horta helped develop art nouveau. Buildings designed in this style often have cast-iron fixtures, stained-glass windows, and many curved lines. About 2,000 art nouveau buildings went up in Brussels alone. Today only about half of them are still standing. One of these is Horta's former home, which is now a museum.

The Atomium lit up at night

Another Brussels landmark is the Atomium. This metal structure was built for the 1958 World Exhibition. At 335 feet (102 m) high, it is one of the tallest buildings in Brussels. The Atomium is a model of an iron molecule and features nine separate ball-shaped compartments. At night, lights bounce off the structure's aluminum coating.

Sweet Sounds

Hundreds of years ago, Belgian church choirs were well known throughout Europe. In more recent times, a number of Belgian composers and performers have become famous for their talents.

A Famous Fountain

A certain small statue in Brussels is famous across Europe. The *Mannekin Pis* shows a young boy urinating. A stone statue of this boy was first displayed in 1619; today's version is made of bronze. In the eighteenth century, French soldiers stole the boy, but the statue was returned to Brussels. To apologize for his soldiers' theft, King Louis XV of France gave the statue a tiny costume. Over the years, hundreds of other outfits have been added to the statue's wardrobe. Today, the Mannekin Pis is often seen wearing one of these costumes, and it is a symbol of the capital city.

A statue dedicated to Adolphe Sax, inventor of the saxophone

The best-known classical composer from Belgium is César Franck. Born in Liège in 1822, he spent most of his adult life writing and teaching music in Paris. Franck was an organist famous for composing tunes off the top of his head—a skill called improvisation. He also wrote symphonies for orchestras. Another nineteenth-century Belgian who made a mark on music was Adolphe Sax. An instrument maker, Sax invented the horn named for him: the saxophone.

Belgians have played a role in modern popular music as well. Django Reinhardt was born in 1910 in Liberchies. As a teen, Reinhardt lost two fingers on his left hand in a fire. Despite this disability, he became one of the greatest jazz guitarists ever. Toots Thielemans, a native of Les Marolles in Brussels, plays jazz harmonica. He also composed the theme song for the TV show *Sesame Street* and has played with such popular American musicians as Paul Simon and Billy Joel.

Jacques Brel was a popular Belgian singer-songwriter. Singing in both French and Flemish, Brel told tales filled with humor and love. During the 1960s, he also sang about social and political trouble, just as folksingers in America did. Although he lived in Paris, Brel often wrote songs about his homeland, and he is still highly regarded there.

Belgian authors tend to write in their native languages, so Belgium has two literary traditions. But when Belgium first won its independence, French was the major literary language, so even Flemish writers used it. One of the best of these Flemish authors who wrote in French was Charles de Coster. His work stirred Walloon writers to develop their own style, rather than merely copying writers from France. De Coster's best-known work is *The Legend of Thyl Ulenspiegel* (1867), based on a Belgian folk hero.

Another Fleming who wrote in French was the poet and playwright Maurice Maeterlinck. His fantasy play *The Bluebird* is still performed today. In 1911, Maeterlinck won the Nobel Prize for Literature.

Today, Belgium's best-known French writers are from Wallonia or Brussels. They include George Simenon and Marguerite Yourcenar. Simenon created the fictional detective Inspector Maigret, who appeared in seventy-six books. Simenon, who died in 1989, wrote hundreds of books during his career. They sold more than 500 million copies around the world, the most ever by a single author. Simenon's work has been translated into more than eighty languages. Yourcenar also wrote novels. She was the first woman named to the Academie Française. This society honors artists and scholars who write in French.

Despite the influence of French on Belgian literature, many Flemings have written important works in their native tongue. One of the first was Hendrik Conscience. His book

The Lion of Flanders (1838) inspired a new interest in Flemish culture. Later in the nineteenth century, the priest Guido Gazelle wrote poetry in Flemish. Much of his work did not become famous until after his death in 1899.

In the twentieth century, Belgium's premier Flemish writer was Hugo Claus. His book *The Sorrow of Belgium* described life in Belgium during World War II. Claus wrote harshly about the Belgians who helped the German Nazis when they occupied Belgium.

On Stage and Screen

Belgian filmmaking and theater feature both Flemish and French. In some cases, English is also used. Although Belgian

A Mix of Art and Words

One popular art is cherished throughout Belgium: the comic strip. And the most popular Belgian comic-strip character is Tintin. This young reporter with a shock of yellow hair has been called the most famous Belgian in the world. The adventures of Tintin and his faithful dog, Milou ("Snowy" in English), have appeared in more than forty languages. In their comics, Tintin and Milou traveled around the world and even into outer space.

Georges Remi, who worked under the name Hergé, created Tintin in 1929. After Hergé died in 1983, no new Tintin comics were created. But the brave reporter and his dog still appear in animated cartoons and on T-shirts. At the Comic Strip Museum, in Brussels, Tintin is the star attraction. The museum, located in a building designed by Victor Horta, features the work of many Belgian comic-strip artists.

Actors on a String

Belgium was once famous for its puppet theaters. Puppets made of wood and papier-mâché acted out classic plays and folktales. Brussels alone once had more than a dozen puppet theaters. Most cities had one puppet that was a famous local character. In Brussels it was Woltje, or "the Little Walloon." Liège had a fellow named Tchantches, and the city has a museum devoted to him and his puppet friends.

Today, Belgium's most famous puppet theater is the Toone (right). Its plays are usually produced in the dialect of Brussels's Les Marolles district. The theater was founded in Les Marolles in 1830, but is now located closer to the Grand Place.

films are not widely shown in the United States, the 1993 film *Daens* was nominated for an Academy Award. In 1997, *Ma Vie en Rose*, about a young Belgian boy and his family, was widely praised. The best-known Belgian movie actor today is Jean-Claude Van Damme. Nicknamed "The Muscles from Brussels," Van Damme uses his skills in karate and kickboxing in his movies. International film star Audrey Hepburn, who died in 1993, was born in Brussels.

As in other countries, theater companies in Belgium have often struggled to receive funding. The best theaters tend to be in the large cities. Theaters in Wallonia perform the works of Belgians who wrote in French, such as Maeterlinck, and translations of works from other languages. Flemish theater thrives in Ghent and Antwerp. Brussels has theater companies devoted to both languages.

Wonder on Wheels

In America, every professional sport has heroes who amaze fans with their talent. In Belgium, the greatest sports hero ever is cyclist Eddy Merckx. Born in 1945, Merckx won cycling's top event, the Tour de France, in 1969. He repeated as champion three more years in a row and won a fifth Tour de France in 1974. Overall, Merckx won more than 140 races, and his success thrilled Belgians across the country. After he retired from racing, Merckx began developing racing bikes.

Although Belgium has produced many great artists, it is less famous for its athletes. But Belgians enjoy playing and watching a number of sports, and their leisure activities include many outdoor pastimes.

Cycling is Belgium's number-one sport. Since most of the country is flat, riding a bike is easy for young and old alike. Belgium has hundreds of miles of cycling paths. The longest one stretches for almost 400 miles (644 km). Taking a leisurely ride is a favorite activity on Sunday afternoons. Some riders belong to local clubs and make cycling a prominent Belgian social event. Belgians also compete in cycling races and rallies. The Tour de Belgium is one of the world's top cycling events.

Another popular sport is soccer. Belgium has a professional league, and amateurs play on club teams. The Belgian national team often competes in the World Cup, the "World Series" of international soccer.

Other popular sports include billiards, jogging, golf, volleyball, and table tennis. A popular spectator sport is motor racing. The Belgian Grand Prix is among the world's top events for Formula One race cars. Many races are held on city streets rather than at racetracks. The most famous Belgian race-car driver is Jackie Ickx. He won the famous race at Le Mans, France, six times and was twice the world sports car champion. Ickx also raced motorcycles, which is popular in Belgium.

Pigeon racing, Belgium's most unusual sport, was developed in Belgium and England. Specially trained pigeons are released miles from their home. Then they are timed to see how long it takes them to return. The pigeons can fly more than 40 miles per hour (64 kph). Pigeon racing is so popular that the times of the birds are broadcast on the radio. Like cycling, pigeon racing offers its fans a social event for a weekend afternoon.

When Belgians want to head outdoors to exercise, they choose from a number of activities. In the summer, many people flock to the North Sea beaches to swim—or just to soak up the sun. Another popular spot is the Ardennes. The forests are great for hiking, camping, fishing, canoeing, and hunting.

Lokonda Mpenza (in white) plays for Belgium at the 1998 World Cup.

Pleasures
of Life

SOME OUTSIDERS CONSIDER BELGIUM SMALL AND UNIM-portant. Other Europeans often joke about Belgians. Even some Belgians feel a little unsure at times about their country's importance. It lacks a long history as an independent nation. Its people are split into two distinct cultures. In 1998, Luc Sante, an American writer born in Belgium, said about his homeland, "It is an awkward child wearing a kick-me sign on its back."

But in their hearts, Belgians love their country. They know its charms, even if many foreigners don't. Belgians believe their country offers them a good life. About two-thirds of the

Belgians like gathering together for festivals.

people own their homes. They have every modern convenience. Belgians have a passion for food and festivals. Others may poke fun at them, but the Belgians know how to enjoy what they have.

Everyday Life

Along with wanting to own their own home, most Belgians seek privacy and space around them. Belgian homeowners like large yards. In apartment buildings, tenants tend to keep to themselves. Belgians may appear to be a little distant to

A scenic manor in Sosoye

A Sweet Sense of Humor

Many Belgians enjoy poking fun at people who are stuffy or take themselves too seriously. "The Pieman" has led the way in this effort, throwing cream pies in the faces of famous people.

The Pieman is Noel Godin, who "creamed" his first victim in 1968. When he's armed with his pies, Godin calls himself George the Glooper. His targets have included artists and government officials. As many as thirty people help Godin track down his victims and greet them with a pie. In 1998, Godin hit his fiftieth target—Bill Gates, the founder of Microsoft and the richest man in the world.

strangers, but they readily show their warmth with their relatives and closest friends. Dropping by to visit someone without calling is rare and might seem a little rude.

In Flanders, many single-family homes have been built since World War II. Homes in Wallonia tend to be older. Modern suburbs ring every major town. The rush to build new homes has meant the end of some farmlands.

In the past, many generations of a family often lived together in one home. Today, more elderly people are moving into senior housing, instead of living with their grown children. And young Belgian families are having fewer children than in the past. The average now is two children per family.

Many families share their home with pets. Dogs, cats, birds, and fish are favorites. Some cities have bird markets on weekend mornings, where people can buy birds and other animals. Over the years, Belgians have bred several types of dogs that are now famous around the world. These include the Belgian shepherd and Belgian Malinois. The Malinois is sometimes trained for use by police.

Belgian shepherds

Dangerous Driving

For years, Belgians were considered some of the worst drivers in Europe. The government first began issuing driver's licenses in the 1960s. At the time, almost anyone over the age of eighteen could get one, no questions asked. Drivers typically ignored road signs and drove at high speeds.

Today, drivers must pass a test to get a license, but accidents are still common. Many drivers tend to follow too closely behind the cars in front of them. Another problem is the *priorité de droite*—French for "priority from the right." On some streets, cars entering from the right side of the road do not have to stop.

On the Road

Although Belgium has excellent public transportation, owning and driving cars is a part of daily life. About 50 percent of the population owns a car. As in America, cars are often a sign of a family's status. People like to drive expensive cars to show their wealth. Belgian cars, however, tend to be smaller than American ones.

The speed limit in Belgium varies, depending on the type of road. On highways, it is 75 miles per hour (120 kilometers per hour). Major country roads have a limit of 56 miles per hour (90 kph), and smaller roads have a 31-miles-per-hour (50 kph) limit. Laws against drunk driving are strict. A person who drives after more than one drink is over the legal limit.

Food, Glorious Food

Something no one jokes about in Belgium is the food. From street carts to formal restaurants, Belgians have many choices for where and what to eat when they dine out. Brussels alone has more than 2,000 restaurants.

"Restaurant Street" is a popular dining area in Brussels.

Belgian waffles are sometimes topped with vanilla ice cream and strawberries.

On the streets of most cities, visitors find small carts and stands selling a favorite sweet treat: Belgian waffles. The waffles come covered with a sugar glaze, dusted with powdered sugar, or topped with ice cream or fruit. The fancier waffles are eaten sitting down, but the basic waffle is meant to be eaten on the run. Another popular food sold at carts is *escargots*—French for snails. The vendor scoops the tiny snails out of hot water and puts them in a paper cup or cone.

Belgian Fries

Americans know them as French fries, but some Belgians claim these strips of fried potato were first made in Belgium. *Frites* are sold on street corners everywhere, and the Belgian fries may be the best in the world. The secret to their taste? They're cooked twice. Vendors fry a batch, then keep the frites in a heap until someone places an order. The fries are then cooked again and served hot and extra crispy. Traditionally, Belgians dipped their frites in mayonnaise. Today, vendors offer a variety of sauces, and some are flavored with curry or other tangy spices. There's something to satisfy almost any taste.

Across Belgium, each region has its specialties. Most meals feature meat or fish. In addition to beef, pork, lamb, and poultry, Belgians enjoy game meat, such as venison (deer), rabbit, and boar. Belgians also eat a variety of fish and seafood, including trout, perch, turbot, shrimp, and eel. One famous Belgian dish is *waterzooi*, Flemish for "hot water." This soup comes originally from Ghent and has either chicken or fish mixed with vegetables.

Brussels is home to a vegetable famous around the world: Brussels sprouts. Another popular vegetable is *witloof*, also called chicory or Belgian endive. The leaves of the witloof are used in salads, and the root can be boiled and served with butter.

One dish popular across Belgium is *moules frites*—mussels and French fries. The mussels are usually served in a broth of wine with garlic, celery, and onion, with the fries on the side.

Crazy for Chocolates

Of all the Belgian food treats, chocolate may top the list. Belgian chocolates are world famous. Some chocolates are made in huge factories. Some are made by hand in small

Opposite: **People eating the popular dish *moules frites*, or mussels and French fries**

A display of Belgian chocolates

shops. Either way, Belgian chocolates are rich and sweet candies. One Belgian cook called chocolates "our national pride."

The typical Belgian chocolate is the praline: a hard chocolate shell with a filling. The filling might be more chocolate, fruit creams, nuts, or a liquid. Another popular chocolate is the *fruits de mer*—French for "fruit of the sea." These seashell-shaped candies are usually a mixture of chocolate and ground hazelnuts. When visiting friends, Belgians often give their hosts a small box of pralines.

Belgians enjoy chocolate in many forms, not just in candy. A popular breakfast item is a piece of bread covered with chocolate paste. Belgians eat this paste the way Americans eat peanut butter. Chocolate milk, made with dark chocolate, is also a Belgian treat.

A Thirst for Beer

Beer is without doubt the national drink of Belgium. The people drink it with their meals and at celebrations. The country's brewers make more than 400 kinds of beer, and many styles are found nowhere else in the world. Each type of beer is served in its own special glass. Belgian beers can be blond, brown, or red, as well as the more usual golden color of most American beers.

Beer making in Belgium goes back more than 1,000 years. During the Middle Ages, monks brewed much of the country's beer. Today, Trappist monasteries still produce some of the best Belgian beers. Although most beer is made from barley, some Belgians brewers also add wheat to their beer.

The Brussels region is home to a special brew called lambic. Vats of beer are left open so wild yeast can fall in. The yeast turns the sugar in the barley into alcohol—and also gives the lambic a distinct taste. Some lambics are also flavored with fruit, such as cherries, raspberries, or peaches.

Festivals and Celebrations

"It only takes three Belgians to make a party." That saying shows how eager Belgians are to celebrate and have a good

Special Celebrations

Weddings and the birth of a child give Belgians good reason to celebrate with friends and family. One Belgian wedding tradition is to auction off the garter, a small band worn on the leg. The winning bidder gets the honor of removing the garter from the bride's leg, and the money raised in the auction goes to the wedding couple.

When a baby is born, the child's godparents give out white, sugar-coated Jordan almonds to friends and relatives. The almonds come in a tiny porcelain baby shoe or another object related to a baby. A card or label with the child's name and birth date is also attached to the shoe.

A group of Gilles participating in the Lenten festivities of Binche

Holidays and Festivals

Many Belgian holidays are celebrated across the nation. Others are just for a certain region or language community.

January 1	New Year's Day
March or April	Easter Monday
Last Saturday of April	Feast Day of the Brussels Region
May 1	Labor Day
May	Ascension Day (sixth Thursday after Easter)
	Whit Monday (seventh Monday after Easter)
July 11	Feast Day of the Flemish Community
July 21	Independence Day
August 15	Assumption Day
Third Sunday in September	Feast Day of the Walloon Region
September 27	Feast Day of the French Community
November 1	All Saints' Day
November 11	Armistice Day
November 15	Feast Day of the German Community and Dynasty Day
December 6	St. Nicholas Day
December 25	Christmas

time. Almost every town has a festival or celebration, often with parades and public dancing. Some of the most famous Belgian festivals are hundreds of years old.

Some Belgian festivals are tied to religious events, such as Lent, which comes in late winter. Others celebrate historic military victories or the changing of the seasons. Binche is famous for its Lenten festival that features dancers called Gilles. The Gilles

Feline Frenzy

The Ypres Cat Festival is an event that honors felines. People dress in giant cat costumes and walk the streets for a parade during the festival. In olden times, however, cats weren't treated with such respect during the celebration. In the Middle Ages, the wool merchants of Ypres kept cats in the winter to kill mice in their warehouses. But in the summer, the city was overrun by cats. To reduce the cat population, the first cat festivals were held. Cats were thrown from buildings and killed. This bloody practice ended in 1817. Now, only cloth cats are thrown.

wear gold uniforms and ostrich feathers in their hats. For part of the day, the dancers wear identical masks painted with a moustache and glasses. As they dance, the Gilles throw oranges into the crowds lining the streets. The oranges are symbols of the coming of spring.

The towns of Heusen and Ath feature annual celebrations with dancers dressed as giants. The Ath celebration dates back to 1390. In today's parade, a male and female giant are married in front of the town hall. Almost any time of the year, in some part of Belgium, a community has something to celebrate.

Timeline

Belgian History

Spain gives the Spanish Netherlands to Austria; the land becomes known as the Austrian Netherlands.	1713
France takes control of Belgium.	1795
Napoléon is defeated at Waterloo; Belgium comes under Dutch control.	1815
Belgium proclaims its independence from the Netherlands.	1830
The nations of Europe accept Belgian independence; Prince Leopold of Saxe-Coburg, a German state, becomes the first king of Belgium.	1831
King Leopold II inherits the throne.	1865
Belgium establishes a colony in the Congo in Africa.	1885
King Albert takes over as head of Belgium.	1909
Germany ignores Belgian neutrality and invades Belgium; the country is the scene of fierce fighting during World War I.	1914
Leopold III ascends to the throne.	1934
Germany again invades Belgium.	1940
The Battle of the Bulge, fought in the Belgian Ardennes, marks a major victory for Allied forces against the Germans.	1944
Belgium becomes a founding member of the North Atlantic Treaty Organization (NATO).	1949
Leopold III steps down from the throne in favor of his son, Baudouin.	1951
Brussels becomes the headquarters of the new European Economic Community (now called the European Union).	1958
Belgium grants the Belgian Congo its independence.	1960
NATO headquarters are moved to Brussels.	1967
A revision to the Belgian constitution creates three cultural communities based on language (Flemish, French, and German) and three geographic regions (Wallonia, Flanders, Brussels).	1970
Parliament creates a federal form of government, giving more local control to Flanders, Wallonia, and Brussels.	1993
King Albert II becomes king of Belgium.	1993

World History

1776	The Declaration of Independence is signed.
1789	The French Revolution begins.
1865	The American Civil War ends.
1914	World War I breaks out.
1917	The Bolshevik Revolution brings Communism to Russia.
1929	Worldwide economic depression begins.
1939	World War II begins, following the German invasion of Poland.
1957	The Vietnam War starts.
1989	The Berlin Wall is torn down as Communism crumbles in Eastern Europe.
1996	Bill Clinton is reelected U.S. president.

Fast Facts

Official name: Kingdom of Belgium

Capital: Brussels

Official languages: Flemish, French, and German

A canal in Bruges

Belgian flag

Seaside at Ostend

Official religion:	None
Founding date:	October 4, 1830, independence from the Netherlands; July 21, 1831, ascension of King Leopold I; July 14, 1993, creation of a federal state
National anthem:	*"La Brabanconne"* ("The Song of Brabant")
Type of government:	Constitutional monarchy
Chief of state:	King
Head of government:	Prime minister
Area:	11,781 square miles (30,510 sq km)
Dimensions:	Southeast–northwest, 174 miles (280 km) Northeast–southwest, 137 miles (220 km)
Bordering countries:	France, the Netherlands, Germany, and Luxembourg
Highest elevation:	Signal de Botrange, in the Ardennes, 2,277 feet (694 m)
Lowest point:	The North Sea, sea level
Average daily temperatures (Brussels):	January: 37°F (3°C) July: 64°F (18°C)

Average annual precipitation:

North Sea	less than 30 inches (76 cm)
Ardennes	more than 40 inches (102 cm)
National average	31 inches (79 cm)

National population (1997 est.): 10,174,922

Population of largest cities in Belgium:

Brussels (metro region)	950,597
Antwerp	453,030
Ghent	225,469
Charleroi	204,899
Liège	189,510
Bruges	115,500
Namur	105,243

Famous landmarks:
- ▶ *Altarpiece, St. Bavo's Cathedral* (Ghent)
- ▶ *Ardennes Forest* (in southeastern Belgium)
- ▶ *Cathedral of Our Lady* (Antwerp)
- ▶ *Grand Place* (Brussels)
- ▶ *Medieval streets and canals of Bruges*

Industry: About 65 percent of the Belgian gross domestic product is tied to the importing and exporting of goods. Raw materials are imported, and finished manufactured goods are sent abroad. Steel production and the manufacture of autos and chemicals are major industries. High-tech industries, such as electronics and biotechnology, are on the rise. About 70 percent of working Belgians are employed in service industries, which include public service, health, education, retail sales, and finance. Major agricultural goods include livestock (cattle, sheep, pigs), grains, and ornamental plants.

Currency: Through 2001, the Belgian franc (BF). 1999 exchange rate: U.S.$1 = 38.16 BF. Starting in 2002, Belgium will use the Euro, a new currency issued in most European Union countries. 1999 exchange rate: U.S.$1 = .95 Euro.

Weights and measures: Metric system

Literacy: 99%

Bruges

Currency

Common Flemish and French phrases:

English	Flemish	French
yes	ja	oui
no	nee	non
please	alstublieft	s'il vous plaît
thank you	dank u	merci
hello (good day)	goedendag	bonjour
good evening	goedenavond	bonsoir
good-bye	tot ziens	au revoir
How are you?	Hoe maakt u het?	Comment allez-vous?
very well	goed	très bien
How much?	Hoeveel?	Combien?
Where is . . . ?	Waar is . . . ?	Où est . . . ?

Famous Belgians:

Albert II *Current king*	(1934–)
Hieronymous Bosch *Painter*	(1450–1516)
Father Damien *Missionary*	(1840–1889)
Leo Hendrik Baekeland *Inventor*	(1863–1944)
Audrey Hepburn *Actress and humanitarian*	(1929–1993)
Georges Remi (Hergé) *Comic-strip artist*	(1907–1983)
Adolphe Sax *Inventor*	(1814–1894)
Jacob van Artevelde *Political revolutionary*	(1295–1345)
Jean-Claude Van Damme *Actor*	(1960–)
Jan van Eyck *Painter*	(1390–1440)

A Tintin comic

To Find Out More

Nonfiction

▶ Birch, Beverly. *Father Damien: Missionary to a Forgotten People.* Milwaukee: G. Stevens Children's Books, 1990.

▶ Bles, Mark. *Child at War: The True Story of a Young Belgian Resistance Fighter.* San Francisco: Mercury House, 1991.

▶ Gaunt, William. *The Golden Age of Flemish Art.* New York: Greenwich House, 1983.

▶ Lerner Department of Geography Staff. *Belgium in Pictures.* Minneapolis: Lerner Publications, 1991.

▶ Muller, Kristine, ed. *Belgium.* London: APA Publications, 1998.

▶ Pateman, Robert. *Belgium.* New York: Marshall Cavendish, 1995.

Multimedia

▶ *The Battle of the Bulge.* Atlas Video, 1989.

Websites

▶ **Belgian Comics**
http://www.geocities.com/paris/cafe/
2877/comics.html
*An unofficial site that offers details
on Tintin and other famous Belgian
comic-strip characters.*

▶ **Belgian Federal
Government Online**
http://belgium.fgov.be
*Provides information about Belgian
government, society, and history.*

▶ **Brussels—Capital Region**
http://www.bruxelles.irisnet.be/
index.htm
*Gives a detailed look at the city of
Brussels and the surrounding region,
with information on politics, history,
and travel.*

▶ **Welcome to Wallonia!**
http://www.wco.com/~sfwallon/
*Provides information on the French-
speaking region of Wallonia.*

Organizations and Embassies

▶ **Embassy of Belgium**
3330 Garfield Street NW
Washington, DC 20008
(202) 333-6900

▶ **Belgian Tourist Office**
780 Third Ave., Suite 1501
New York, NY 10017
(212) 758-8130

▶ **Wallonia Trade Office**
Belgian Trade Commission
595 Market St., Suite 2500
San Francisco, CA 94105
(415) 546-5255

Index

Page numbers in *italics* indicate illustrations.

Meet the Author

MICHAEL BURGAN got his first glimpse of Belgium when he was eighteen. "I was backpacking with two friends across Europe. We spent a rainy Sunday morning at one of Brussels's stations waiting for a train to the Netherlands. It took me another twenty years to come back and see what Brussels and Belgium were really all about."

When he returned to Belgium in 1998, Burgan appreciated the country's great artistic tradition. He also met Belgians eager to discuss their country and its history. And he sampled one of the world's greatest sweets: Belgian chocolate. His experiences as a traveler in Belgium helped shape this book. But so did hours of research.

"I used the Internet, which gave me access to Belgian government sites. I also found sites devoted to Belgian *frites* and comic strip characters. Newspapers and magazines on the Web

gave me the latest reports on Belgian news events. In the library, I found books on Flemish art, the language disputes between Walloons and Flemings, and Belgium's many years of foreign rule. I also talked to a native Belgian living in the United States. She gave me information on cultural traditions that I didn't find anywhere else."

Burgan worked as an editor at *Weekly Reader* for six years before becoming a freelance writer. He has written more than twenty books for children and young adults, both fiction and nonfiction. His other titles for Children's Press include *Argentina* and *England*, for the True Books series, and *Maryland*, for the America the Beautiful series. He has a BA in history and studied playwriting for one year. In his spare time, he enjoys theater, films, music, and travel.

Photo Credits

Photographs ©:

AllSport USA: 115 (Agence Vandystadt), 114 (Mike Powell);
Archive Photos: 41, 43, 49;
Art Resource, NY: 100 (National Gallery, London, Great Britain/Photograph by Erich Lessing), 108 (Musée Horta, Brussels, Belgium/Photograph by Erich Lessing);
Belgian National Tourist Office: 113 (L. Dennis), 7 bottom, 30 (Michael M. Fairchild), 32 (Marvullo), 19, 22 bottom, 53, 88, 95, 124, 127;
Bridgeman Art Library International Ltd., London/New York: 101 (BAL4096/Rogier van der Weyden, 1399-1464, Portrait of a Lady, c. 1450-60, oil on panel/National Gallery, London, UK.);
Corbis-Bettmann: 69 (Underwood & Underwood), 47 (UPI);
Dan Polin: 93;
Envision: 121 bottom (Ed Bishop), 105 (Jack Casement);
Liaison Agency, Inc.: 59 (Didier Lebrun/Photo News), 56 (Photo News), 13 (Diana Walker), 55;
Nance S. Trueworthy: 73;
North Wind Picture Archives: 34, 35, 37, 38, 45;
Peter Arnold Inc.: 119 (Gerard Lacz);
Photo Researchers: 28 top (Manfred Danegger/OKAPIA), 109 (Philippart De Foy), 126 (Jose Dupont/Explorer), 31 (Jacques Jangoux), 27 (Gail Jankus), 22 (Ronny Jaques), 28 bottom (Tom McHugh), 62 (Sam C. Pierson, Jr.), 8, 106, 130 (Porterfield/Chickering), 26 (John Tinning);
Robert Fried Photography: 12 top, 78, 80, 83, 96 top, 116;
Stock Montage, Inc.: 36, 90;
Superstock, Inc.: 33 (Christie's Images), 102 (Kunsthistorisches Museum, Vienna, Austria), 104 (Private Collection, Brussels, Belgium/Lauros-Giraudon, Paris), cover, 6, 18, 20, 23, 51, 74, 86;
The Image Works: 9, 21 top, 65, 122 (B. Roland), 71 top, 87 (Lee Snider);
Tiofoto: 75, 121 top (Nils-Johan Norenlind), 64 (Jan Rietz);
Tony Stone Images: 7 bottom, 17 (Philip H. Coblentz), 52 (David Hanson), 63 (David Hughes), 107 (Will & Deni McIntyre), 98 (Steve Vidler);
Topham Picturepoint: 66, 70, 132 bottom;
Ulrike Welsch: 25, 99;
Victor Englebert: 10, 12 bottom, 14, 15, 24, 29, 40, 61, 67, 68, 84, 85, 91, 94, 96 bottom, 110, 112, 118, 131, 132 top, 133;
Viesti Collection, Inc.: 76, 117 (Joe Viesti);
Visuals Unlimited: 71 bottom (James Alan Brown).
Maps by Joe LeMonnier.